What's Left of Me

How I lost a fight with a rogue hippo and won my life

PAUL TEMPLER

Ever onward!
Cheers, Paul Templer.

Hawkings Post

What's Left of Me
How I lost a fight with a rogue hippo and won my life
by Paul Templer

Editorial Director: Rebecca J. Ensign
Assistant Editor: Nathan Thomson
Contributing Editor: Chris Walton

Cover art: Patrick VanLehn
Cover and book design: Tony Boisvert; Boisvert Design

Templer, Paul.
  What's left of me : how I lost a fight with a rogue hippo and won my life / by Paul Templer.
    p. cm.
  ISBN 978-1-938881-00-8 (938881)
  1. Templer, Paul 2. Safari guides--Zimbabwe--Biography. I. Title.
  G516.T45A3 2012
  916.8910092--dc23
  [B]
                        2012029501

Published by Hawkings Post, a division of opusdynamic
www.hawkingspost.com

For permissions, ordering information or inquiries, contact:
Hawkings Post; Detroit, MI; (313) 737-3373; orders@hawkingspost.com

ISBNs: Hard cover: 978-1-938881-00-8
        Ebook: 978-1-938881-01-5; $12.99

$24.95; Hard cover; 240 pages

10 9 8 7 6 5 4 3 2 1

Dedication

To my family. Thank you! I love you! IGB.

Contents

What's Left of Me

How I lost a fight with a
rogue hippo and won my life

Paul Templer

Chapter 1

The Early Years

Rhodesia
Summer 1978

I could taste the dirt. That and the weird metal taste that fills your mouth when you're scared, really scared. Sweat stung my eyes and my cracked feet burnt on the sun- scorched earth. My discomfort was nothing compared to my fear. I was scared of so many things, but as a nine-year-old child of Africa, I knew that showing fear wasn't an option. Even as the young lion stalked me in that makeshift arena, I refused to let either him, or our audience, know how scared I really was. I glanced up at the faces staring at me, faces contorted with excitement as they took a break from their normal business of dealing death. Black faces, white faces, camouflage outfits, bullets, guns, white teeth, and their eyes. I was surrounded by predators.

I had taken the long and dangerous drive to visit my dad who was stationed on a military base in what was then Rhodesia. The drive was made dangerous by the real threat of an ambush by the "terrs", Communist terrorists who were trying to take over our country.

I was planning on spending some time with my dad, a senior officer in the Rhodesian Army and his troops, some of the fiercest, finest and bravest warriors ever to don a military uniform. These were the men of the Rhodesian African Rifles.

As a nine-year-old, I had a very basic understanding of the world. As far as I knew, the world had always been at war. Our country had problems, and since we weren't handling our problems the way the rest of the world wanted, we were the bad guys. Meanwhile, the terrs were trying to kill us all so that they could take over the country. "Terrs" was short for terrorists, which is what they were to us. But, the rest of the world seemed to see them as freedom fighters and supported them. I agreed with the grown-ups. "Fuck the rest of the world!"

My dad spent most of his time away from home with his men trying to stop the terrs from taking over our country. If I ever wanted to see him, my choices were quite simple; I would either take the dangerous trip and run the risk of being ambushed, or I just didn't get to see him.

Of course, I chose to go to see him, which is why I found myself in the middle of a makeshift gladiator arena, stalked by an orphaned young lion.

It was cub versus cub. The lion cub had recently been adopted by the regiment after a platoon who'd been out on patrol followed some vultures and found the cub lying next to his dead mother.

My stock had risen a few years earlier when running around near naked with all the other kids at a regimental Christmas party, I'd fallen into an open cask of millet beer. Instead of drowning, I somehow got myself out of that mess and lived to tell the tale. My reckless nature, undisguised hero-worship of the troops, and apparent invincibility endeared me to the men, and on that day in December, a legend was born.

Anyway, here we were, two adopted sons in the gladiator's arena. The cub was obviously enjoying himself a lot more than I was. His natural instincts erupted in his young muscular body as he stalked me. Were nature to run its course, I knew that I'd be his meal. As clearly as if it were yesterday, I remember staring into his eyes and sharing a brief moment of communication. It was as if he were saying, "You're mine." And then he pounced – this was only the first of many incidents in which a wild animal threatened my life.

In a blur of fur and dust, it didn't take long for the cub to draw first blood and evoke true terror in me. Fortunately, when they thought that I'd had enough, the troops rescued me. My main concern at the time was to save face. That's to say, I didn't want to cry. I picked myself up, shook myself free of the helping hands, and then, eyes staring straight ahead, lip quivering, I walked as proudly as I possibly could to the latrine. I took a moment to pull myself together.

As I stood there, safely away from the cub that tried to rip me to pieces, I felt a sudden and searing pain shoot from my big toe up my foot and into my leg. Satan! Another orphan who'd been rescued by the regiment. He was a mean crow with a bad attitude. He walked around the place as if he owned it. Stinking of the garbage he fed on, the nasty little bugger had snuck up behind me and bitten me.

To that point, I'd managed to act tough, but then the dam burst and I cried. I cried from the terror of my encounter with the cub. I cried from the shame of defeat in front of these men whom I idolized. I cried because Satan had just bitten me on my big toe, and I cried because I was just a little kid and little kids cry.

I pulled myself together and walked out into the sun, shoulders back, head up, facing the world head on just like I'd been taught by Mum and dad. That afternoon I was spoiled rotten. Some of the troopies took me to the range where I got to shoot all sorts of guns – pistols, rifles, and machine-guns. I got pretty good at shooting guns which was a good skill to develop when there were lots of people running around trying to kill you.

That night, with a proudly bruised shoulder from my time on the range, a bruised toe from Satan, and scrapes and cuts from my duel with the lion, I sat on the verandah at the Baobab Hotel, sipping on an ice cold

Coke and nibbling on salt n' vinegar chips. As a nine-year-old, I didn't think that life could get much better than this – until the very next day.

My dad and I set off for Victoria Falls. We took a handful of troopies who were being sent up there with us, just in case the terrs ambushed us along the way. I'd only heard of Victoria Falls at that point. It was a place where the Zambezi River rushed over the mile-long, 300-foot-high precipice before crashing below in the Batoka Gorge sending plumes of mist hundreds of feet up into the air; it was an incredible sight. I spent most of the first day with my dad looking at cannons and gun placements that pointed north towards a staging post used by Joshua Nkomo and his ZIPRA terrorists.

Getting to spend a day with my dad, surrounded by wild animals and Army guys was an awesome time. When we were done for the day, we dropped off the troopies at their barracks and my dad took us to the Victoria Falls Hotel where we got to spend the night. I'd never experienced anything quite like it – tuxedoed waiters, chandeliers, and chocolates on my pillow. I got to swim in the pool, munch on cucumber sandwiches, and wolf down cups of tea and scones with clotted cream and dollops of strawberry jam. Remembering the mist rising above the Falls, I have to agree with Scottish explorer, David Livingstone when he declared "Scenes so lovely as this must have been gazed upon by angels in their flight."

Sadly, all good things have to come to an end, and so the time arrived when we had to leave. As we walked towards my dad's Army Land Rover, we passed a Red Cross ambulance with a couple of chaps sorting some stuff out. Of course I was inquisitive, so my dad took me over and we introduced ourselves to Andre Tieche and Alain Bieri, two young Swiss nationals who were out in Rhodesia working for the Red Cross.

That night, after a long trip back from the falls, I returned to the loving embraces of my other heroes, my Mum and my little sister Lisa, whom I adored.

Not too long after that, we were watching the news and there was a story about two chaps from the Red Cross, Andre Tieche and Alain Bieri, who whilst driving their Red Cross van had been stopped and then brutally murdered by the terrs. It turned out that they, along with their translator Charles Chatora, had been driving around the countryside in their white truck with huge red crosses emblazoned on the sides and rear. They were assessing the medical needs of some of the locals en route to distributing a bale of blankets they'd brought along for people in need. Tragically, they were ambushed and killed. The terrs didn't stop there. They went on to rob them, taking everything including their shoes.

I hated the terrs a little more that night. But even more, I thought of Andre and Alain, and I prayed that they hadn't been too scared or felt too much pain when they died. I thought of their mothers, and I prayed that they would be alright.

The next day the sun rose, and for me anyway, life went on. I got up and went to school. Mum would see us off at the gate and Lisa and I made our way to the corner to meet up with all the other kids; then at 7 o'clock on the dot, we'd all climb aboard a Rhino, a locally manufactured armored personnel carrier which would take us into town. The armed Military Policemen who rode with us were responsible for getting us there alive and in one piece. Each of the Military Policemen was different from each other. Some were really cool and others, in a little boy's mind, were way too uptight.

For me, school was always something to be survived. I was average in the classroom. It wasn't because I couldn't perform well; I was lazy and preoccupied with other interests.

I loved to play sports. As a four-and-a-half-year-old, I had boxing gloves laced up onto my hands for the first time. I won that bout by TKO. I got a clean hit right across my opponent's nose. I showed no mercy, and I reveled in the competition. In the years ahead, I swam competitively, played water polo, rugby, cricket, tennis, squash, soccer, and golf. But no matter the sport, I always took competition seriously.

I got very used to winning, and it made me feel invincible. But then, I learned an incredibly valuable lesson. I'd taken up Judo and was really enjoying it. I started to think I was pretty good at it too. One day when my dad was in town, I invited him to come and witness what I thought would be my rise to glory in the Judo world.

I laughed a little inside when I found out I would be competing against a girl. The fight began. I'd never felt more confident in my entire life. She completely dominated me! She whipped and flipped me about like an almost empty sack of potatoes and then pinned me down. I couldn't move and could hardly breathe. My neck and right arm felt as if they were being slowly pried away from the rest of my body as she went for a submission.

Lying on the ground, pinned by this Judo master, I could only see a small portion of the crowd. But sure enough, right in the middle of my line of vision, I saw my dad, his eyes boring into mine, willing me to do something, anything. I tapped once, twice and then a third time. She leapt off me, reveling in victory, and my pride imploded.

Baron Pierre de Coubertin, the father of the modern Olympics once said "The important thing in life is not victory, but combat; it is not to have vanquished but to have fought well." But I liked winning, and losing sucked. So long, Judo.

Life soon returned to normal. Normal at that time was going to school in an armored personnel carrier with armed Military Policemen who were there because of the impending threat of ambush by the terrs. Normal was driving in convoy if you wanted to travel between the towns. Normal was hours spent on rifle ranges making sure that I could shoot straight.

We did get to do some kid stuff. We spent hours at the stables waiting for an opportunity to escape, galloping bareback into the bush as soon as the adults turned their backs.

The one adult who liked to ride with us was Tex. Tex had arrived in Rhodesia after having served in the Vietnam War. Tex was a country boy with a cowboy saddle and a pair of polished revolvers. He loved horses, and hated Communists. We loved it when Tex would ride with us and tell us stories about his faraway home.

A time came when Tex stopped showing up. That's what some people did in a war. They stopped showing up. It was normal.

When I look back at those early years, I look at them through a child's eyes. They were fun from a little boy's point of view; guns, horses, soldiers, school friends, lazy warm afternoons, ice cold Cokes and toasted sandwiches.

More than anything else, I remember laughing. It was that laughter that wells up deep inside, and then it erupts making your tummy hurt and your nose itch. It was the kind of laughter that shouts "God, it's great to be alive!"

Then there was the flipside. There were many times when we would cry. Sometimes the sadness made it hard to imagine that the sun could rise another day. It was a life of extremes, and extremes were normal.

Amidst this "normal" life, one not so normal night stands out. It began with a knock at the window; it was more like a scrape. Petrified that it was the terrs coming to get me, I snuck up to take a look outside. I felt flooded by relief when I saw that it was Norah, my nanny. She urged me with restrained fear, "Picanin baas, please call the Madam." It wasn't a strange thing to say except that it was the middle of the night, well past curfew, and she had an axe planted squarely in her head! She didn't bother to explain the axe. She told me that it was not a story she could tell to someone so young, but she needed me to find help.

This was only the first problem. The next problem was figuring out how to wake Mum without getting shot. Mum, who slept with an Uzi and a 9mm pistol, was one of the best shots in the whole wide world, and if she were startled in her sleep, I feared she might wake up shooting, especially if she thought her little ones might be in trouble. Luckily, I managed to wake Mum up carefully, and after seeing what state Norah was in, Mum called some troopies who came and took Norah to the hospital.

After that, I didn't see Norah again for a while. Sometime later, Peter, the gardener and the one chap who didn't seem to mind playing with me for hours on end, left us to go and join the Regiment. We'd see him occasionally, but then he stopped showing up, too.

People stopped showing up for lots of reasons, but some reasons were more permanent than others. If someone's dad ever got shot, Mum would visit the mom. Mum would go with the priest and if there were kids, she'd take us. That was really sad and everyone always seemed to end up crying. Events like this made me familiar with people no longer showing up, but I never became okay with it.

There were a few other things that really didn't make much sense to me, like why the Americans, French and British were fighting against us and why they wanted us to give our country to the communists. Didn't they know that the Russians and the Chinese and the North Koreans were baddies?

Then there was the whole black/white thing. I could see firsthand the inequalities – the fact that whites were treated better in the shops than the blacks. We mostly drove cars and they mostly walked, rode bikes or took the busses. We were "baas" or "madam" and they were "Gardener" or "Nanny". We didn't go to the same schools. In town, we really didn't mix much at all. They were generally more polite to us than we were to them except for the ones who were trying to kill us.

But what made it most confusing was the terrs. They were mostly black, except for the Russians who were white and the Chinese who were neither black nor white. We had the troopies on our side, who were also mostly black. In fact, about seventy per cent of our Army was made up of blacks, most of whom were volunteers. The remainder was made up of whites, coloreds, Indians, and Asians. Some were conscripted whilst some volunteered. A handful of soldiers enlisted as fortune and adventure seekers. They came from all around the world. They came from as far as Dallas, Texas and Paris, France.

It was all very confusing. One thing was clear though; the terrs didn't discriminate. They killed everyone – blacks, whites, Indians, Asians, rich, poor, townies, farmers, foreigners, local folk, the moms, the dads, the grandparents, kids, and even babies. It was a normal part of our lives, and that was why we were fighting the war. If the world chose to condemn us, then I agreed with the adults again. "They could all just go and fuck 'emselves." Surely sooner or later they'd come around and see our situation as it really was.

I remember the day that particular dream died. We once had a conviction that the world would see our situation for what it was. But one day, that light was extinguished once and for all.

It was the night of September 3rd, 1978. I was nine, about two weeks short of ten. Mum seemed weird that night. It wasn't a sad weird, but more of an angry weird. The next day at the corner, standing in the sun, waiting for the Rhino Armored Personnel Carrier to take us to school, all us kids were talking about the plane, Hunyani, an Air Rhodesia Viscount on a scheduled civilian passenger flight that was shot down by terrs using a SAM-7 heat-seeking missile. Incredibly, some survived the crash, but they were only safe for a few moments; the miracle negated when all of the survivors were found and murdered by the terrs. When I look back, I think that might have been the day that hope and respect for the West truly died in Rhodesia.

Zimbabwe

Very Rev. John da Costa, Anglican Dean of Salisbury, delivered a sermon at the funeral service for those slain during the terrs' plane attack. His sermon summed up the way a lot of people in that little piece of Africa felt at that time; and I dare say, the sentiment he expressed is deeply relevant and appropriate to today's world in which many seem to be more concerned with forwarding their own agendas with seemingly little consideration for the consequences.

The sermon was called "The Silence is Deafening". I consider it one of the most powerful speeches I've ever been privileged to hear. If you're interested, the sermon has been placed in its entirety at the end of this book.

Things got really grim for a few years as we got on with the business of trying to win the war, or survive it at least. As the war escalated, the atrocities became more commonplace; no one was safe.

Many days and many lives later, Zimbabwe Rhodesia was born. Bishop Abel Muzorewa was to head the government of national unity. Racial integration was now a reality in all spheres of Zimbabwe Rhodesian life, from the military to education, from healthcare to housing and everything in-between. We had tentatively taken another step down the road to democracy. Things were not perfect, but all agreed, this was the way to the future everyone dreamt of.

But the war didn't stop like it was supposed to. It seemed the rest of the world hadn't quite finished playing chess in Africa just yet, and we were still a pawn in play. Sanctions weren't lifted. The terrs still had support from everyone and we still headed the world's Shit List.

By this time, we'd moved to Salisbury. Dad's job needed him there in Joint High Command. Dad seemed sad to leave his job and his men; he loved them. We were glad for the change because we got to see dad more. Plus, we all figured there was less chance of him getting killed if he were in town.

Between September and December 1979, all the politicians met in England at a place called Lancaster House where the British brokered a peace agreement. Our side was led by Bishop Abel Muzorewa and the former Rhodesian Prime Minister, Ian Smith. The terrs were led by Mugabe and Nkomo. They said a lot of great things in those meetings.

There were going to be free and fair elections; one man, one vote.

Consciences appeased, the British were ecstatic, but many of them having never stepped foot in Zimbabwe Rhodesia, had no idea how things really worked there. We had our election; an election that was declared free and fair by all the international observers who came to witness the historic event. However, free and fair Africa style meant that the winning party was the one that intimidated the most people.

It was a couple of weeks before our new Prime Minister, His Excellency, the Right Honorable, Comrade Robert Gabriel Mugabe, President for Life, was enthroned; given the keys to the jewel of Africa by the heir to the British throne, Prince Charles. Immediately after the ceremony, Bob Marley and the Wailers had been invited to perform for an exclusive audience of assembled dignitaries, media and party faithful. This annoyed the general population who wanted to hear their hero belt out the tunes that had earlier inspired them.

Bob Marley and the Wailers' first performance in Zimbabwe was marred by tear gas and chaos. Bob Marley wasn't the only one subdued that night. A new chapter in our country's history had begun and we were left with little doubt that it was going to take a leap of faith to continue living in Zimbabwe. We needed to put aside our worst fears that tear gas, police brutality, rape, murder, pillage and wanton destruction lay ahead. It was time to get on with life as best we could.

Around about Independence, I remember sitting in the lounge on the carpet, playing cards. I was on my very best behavior as I'd been warned that if I messed about, there'd be hell to pay. Talk about an uptight situation! My dad was hosting a luncheon; in attendance were all the head terrs, some of the top Zimbabwe Rhodesia Army people, and some of my folk's friends.

Everyone was playing nicely together when there was one of those pregnant pauses in the conversation; one of those unnatural moments at a gathering when no one speaks.

My voice pierced the silence, "So you're a terr, huh? I've never seen a real live one." I said to the former guerilla Military Commander.

A few very long seconds ticked by; no one seemed to know what to do or to say. Looking around the room, you'd have thought that I'd pulled the pin off a grenade and was sitting there messing about with it.

"No Paul, I am a Zimbabwean," he replied in his deep throaty voice.

Hmmm …

I got to thinking what it means to be a Zimbabwean, a child of Africa, 'cause that's what I am. I'm an African. I was born there, as were generations before me. There are many tribes in Africa and I'm of the white tribe.

When my descendants came to the Dark Continent, they came for a lot of different reasons. They arrived at different times from different places. They were of British descent – English, Irish and Welsh. Some of them had come straight to Africa whilst others had come via New Zealand.

Mum's dad, Richard "Dickie" Scrase had something of a wild side. Having survived being shot down in his fighter plane during World War II, he went on to serve as a flight instructor in the Royal Rhodesian Air Force. Dickie's friends tell of him being the first to loop-the-loop in what was then Rhodesian airspace. They talk of him owning the first sports car in Salisbury, the capital of Rhodesia, and they tell other stories of his general hell-raising.

Mum's memories of him are somewhat different. She remembers joining him from boarding school for the holidays as they'd stump the virgin bush (jungle). Over the years, they built a productive farm, Shambutungwe, with a school and a clinic for the workers. She remembers camping besides swollen rivers during the rainy season as they tried to get into town, sailing off to school in England, and holidaying in Switzerland. Sadly, her somewhat idyllic life ended all too abruptly. When she was just eight years old, her mother got ill and died and then a few years later, her dad died, too. Fortunately, Flora and Donald Hawkings, friends and neighbors who'd been business partners with my grandpa Richard, adopted my Mum and welcomed her into their home and their family.

Dad's dad, Edward "Jock" Templer was an Olympic caliber hurdler and international standard rugby player who spent his prime years, not on an athletic track or rugby pitch, but instead in North Africa in a tank dueling with Rommel and Co. in the desert. After the war, he moved from South Africa to Rhodesia and there he got to live out his dream alongside his wife Jean and their two sons John and Mick. He loved his garden and he loved his family. He was a good, humble man who inspired people to be all that they wished to be.

Through the years, all of my descendants who came and stayed there endured all that Africa could throw at them. It started when they first arrived, standing on the deck of a sailing ship. The expanse of blue sea and sky was separated only by hue and then replaced by the cloud topped Table Mountain. They ventured off; some joined wagon trains, others settled in mining towns, or built farms out of the virgin bush that they painstakingly, lovingly transformed into a source of livelihood – full crops of maize, tobacco, bananas and paprika. Cattle grazed and children ran barefoot through the lands. They withstood gunshots, snake-bites, wild animal attacks, farm invasions, ambushes, mines collapsing, car wrecks, plane crashes, piracy, malaria, bilharzia, alcoholism, cancer, heart attacks, day-long parties, and night-long soirées.

Fortunes were made, fortunes were lost, and fortunes were made again. People fell in love, fell out of love, stayed faithful, had affairs, and the family continued to grow and survive and overcome trials and tribulations; each challenge making the family a little stronger, rooting in a little deeper. Some left Africa and others stayed. With ties to Great Britain, both of my grandpas served the Crown in the "War to end all Wars". Unfortunately, circumstances dictated that most of their descendants were forced to leave our home in Africa as our worst fears at independence were sadly realized.

When I close my eyes and open my mind, I can still smell the rain, taste the dust, and feel the camaraderie of the people. Life is hard in Africa; if you let yourself, you can taste it when they open the airplane door and the air rushes in. You can see it in the eyes of her sons and daughters. What is the essence of Africa? I don't know that words can convey it. I certainly don't have them. Some say that life is cheap, and that might be so. Watch the news and witness the brutality, but it is also true that it is precious. Watch the news and witness the tenderness.

Perhaps that's the essence. It's a land of contrasts. Everything has its time and everything has its place. It's almost as if we take our cue from the environment. Take for example, the pride of lions that chase down an old buffalo. A well-placed, powerful bite from one of the lions breaks the buffalo's spine, and immobilizes the animal so that it can be eaten. It's a brutal scene when witnessed as an isolated incident, but if we keep watching, we'll see that the pride gets to eat; the moms, the dads, the cubs, then the scavengers – the hyenas and the vultures – come and clean up whatever's left. The animals don't act without a reason. Everything has a time, a place, and a purpose.

But we often act as if we've forgotten this. I find it alarming that, having evolved into civilized human beings, we treat each other so poorly. Maybe we need to pay a little more attention to the way that wild animals coexist with one another, the way that they take care of one another, work together for the betterment of the group as a whole. They work together to survive, and if they choose not to, they die.

Growing Up

When I was eleven years old my parents got divorced. I was convinced that it was all my fault. I was sure that if I could just have been a better kid, then they would have been happy and stayed together. I didn't believe them when they told me that it really wasn't about me. I'd done everything I could in the years leading up to the divorce. I'd excelled at sports, and worked hard in the classroom but it hadn't been enough. So once they got the divorce I decided, "To hell with it all." My grades dropped in the classroom, I put no effort into sports, my attitude sucked and I was rather unpleasant to be around. I was self-destructing and I was doing it fast.

It took saintly patience for Mum to put up with me. As a single mother, she struggled to make ends meet. She seemed to work every hour that God sent her and at the same time, she was back at school learning so that she could more effectively follow her calling, working with the mentally and physically disabled. She got no support from me. I was revolting. I was rude, obnoxious, lazy, and downright mean. Thank goodness my sister Lisa was there for Mum. Lisa was a blessing in our family. She has always been wise beyond her years and has had an incredible sense of compassion tinged with a wicked sense of humor.

After the divorce, Mum, Lisa and I lived together; dad had moved out and then it seemed it was my turn. I was off to boarding school. Father O'Halloran, the Rector of Saint Georges, and Mum decided that I needed to be saved from myself and that a Catholic boarding school was just what was needed.

When I look back at our situation, there was no way that our family could afford for me to go to boarding school, neither could we afford for me not to, so I went. This was what was so infuriating about Mum's and Lisa's approach to life. They kept on telling me that it was real simple. If I just worked hard, did the next right thing and kept on showing up, things would work out the way they were meant to. It was infuriating only because it stole all of my excuses.

So, in 1981, the year after our country changed her name to Zimbabwe, I went to Saint Georges, the boarding school we referred to as "Saints". It was a Roman Catholic school that had first opened its doors in 1896. I thought that it was the best school in the country. Saints oozed history. There was a castle, with the turret serving as the centerpiece, that sat on top of a hill and was surrounded by classrooms, dormitories, sports fields and manicured gardens. Saints had a proven track record, producing many of our country's leaders and, as students, we gained a contagious confidence that bordered on arrogance. It didn't always make us very popular with kids from other schools, but we were okay with that.

It was an eclectic bunch that gathered that year. My classmates included the nephew of the Prime Minister, the son of the Vice President and various other politicos' offspring. There were townies' kids and there were farmers' kids. Some were boarders and some were day scholars. The staff was as diverse as the students. Some were new and some were old, some of the cloth and others laity.

On our first day going through the roster, Colonel Lind got to the name Elliott and said, "Elliott, Sean Elliott, any relation to Ant Elliott?"

"Son, Sir" Sean replied.

When he got to the T's, Colonel Lind said, "Templer, Paul Templer, any relation to John Templer?"

"Son, Sir," I replied.

There was a pause; the Colonel lifted his head, his eyes scanning the room, settling on Sean and I, he said "Young men, I taught both your fathers." And to me that summed up Saints, some things changed and some things didn't.

One constant was that when you went astray, there was a series of prescribed remedies designed to bring you back onto the straight and narrow. The school was structured quite simply; there were about four hundred students between the ages of twelve and eighteen, and about half of the students were boarders. The remainder were day scholars. Class sizes varied but there would seldom be a class with more than twenty or so students to a teacher.

There were four houses; "house" is the collective noun for a group of students. Houses would compete against each other in sports, academics and social pursuits (e.g. public speaking). The day-to-day running of the school was left to the senior students who themselves were led by the Head Boy, his two Deputies (one for boarders, one for day scholars), Prefects, and House Prefects. Writing Lines, Manual Labor or "having a good talking to" could be prescribed by the Head Boy and his cohorts. A "Smokers Workout" was the most extreme punishment that could be administered by the student body, but only for the most heinous of offenses, such as bringing the school's name and reputation into disrepute.

Only the teachers could prescribe beatings, which came in the form of ferulas or canings. Ferula's were beatings to the hands and canings were lashings on the bottom. Most of the beatings that I received I totally deserved so I've no complaints.

What I liked about the discipline at school was that it was tied into a very clearly defined game. If you worked within the prescribed guidelines, all was well, but boys will be boys and we obviously bent the rules from time to time. We would push the limits and sometimes we'd go too far. When caught, we'd be punished and then our slate would be clean and the world would be a good place again. I'm not suggesting that this works for everybody, but it worked for me as it provided clear cause and effect in my life.

Clarity and consistency became the hallmarks of my daily existence. Revallie was at six in the morning when we'd line up and be marched through to shower. We then had about fifteen minutes to get dressed before lining up to enter the dining halls for breakfast. Silence followed by prayers started and ended every meal, each of which served to us by waiters. Assembly was at eight o'clock in the morning with classes through lunchtime in Latin, English, History, Mathematics, Music, the Sciences, Modern Languages, Economics, the Arts, Religion and Physical Education.

We returned to the dining halls for lunch at one o'clock, back for more questionable cuisine and tea rumored to be laced with saltpeter, which apparently was meant to keep us from getting horny. Some days, we had classes in the afternoon. Every school day plus Saturday we had sport. There were the dreaded house workouts led by the seniors that occasionally ended up with some kids crying and throwing up.

Then there were official school sports – Track and Field, Cross Country, Swimming, Water Polo, Tennis, Squash, Rowing, Cricket, Rugby, Field Hockey, and Soccer. Participation in a sport was mandatory. There were also clubs – Shooting Club, Astronomy, Weight Lifting, Adventurers, Debating, and Computers. At five o'clock it was tea time, then studies through 'till seven o'clock with an optional half hour Mass for good measure.

After supper, there was half an hour to either relax, take a beating if you had one due, or "have a good talking to" by the Seniors up in their Senior Common Room or the Prefects at Prefects Room. Then it was back to the study hall where another period of enforced silence provided the opportunity to get homework done before returning to the dorm for a brief social unwind period. Then it was time for showers and fifteen minutes of silence to read before lights out. Another day would soon start with the bell announcing the six o'clock reveille.

This was the basic routine of the next six years of my life. I loved it, and I believe it was the very best thing that could have happened to me; it provided the necessary structure and discipline to a kid who was totally out of control.

Midway through my Saints career, as a young teenager, I got really sick. I was diagnosed with Chronic Glomerulonephritis, or as I put it, my kidneys went "kaput". The doctors told us that it was caused by bilharzia, a waterborne parasite that most people who live in Africa will pick up at some point in time. You get it from swimming in dams. If it attacks your kidneys, it manifests itself through excruciating pain in the lower back, scarily high blood pressure and blood in the urine. My prognosis was not good, death a likely possibility. I was worried of course, but thanks to the medication, my pain was well managed which left me feeling okay, but bored beyond belief.

The Catholic Hospital was staffed in part by nuns, with the remainder laity. They were very good to me, which in hindsight is quite remarkable as I was a complete pain in their collective arses. During the months that I was laid up, I made numerous acquaintances. There was the old bloke who came into the hospital to get his appendix out and ended up leaving without a leg. Then there was the alcoholic ex-troopie who had bad dreams and was in with an ulcer. He would wheel me around the hospital gardens in my wheelchair and teach me how to track people and animals.

There were some lads my age; Badza is one who stands out in my memory. He was there to get his diabetes managed and was about as thrilled as I was to be locked up. At night, once the lights went out, we'd stuff our beds so that it would appear that we were fast asleep. Then we'd nip out through the bathroom window and go play. Usually we'd head down to Happy Days, a nearby fast food joint that specialized in greasy burgers or we'd head to The George, a rather sleazy hotel where we could get something to drink. Sometimes we'd just sit on a rock, smoke cigarettes and revel in the illicitness of the moment.

One night, returning from a solo mission, I crawled through the bars on the window only to come face to face with Father Nixon. He was my dormitory master at school and a legend in his own lifetime. Whilst renowned for being indisputably fair, much of his legend was derived from his prowess with the whipping cane. He and my dad had clashed a generation ago and had both emerged with a grudging respect for one another. He was disarmingly calm as he took me back to my ward, where Nurse Sally and Sister Agatha were waiting, and very pissed.

Sister Agatha was a nun. Germanic in accent and in nature, she was incredibly efficient and to the point. She scared the hell out of me with her "no nonsense" manner. Nurse Sally was young, brunette, nice, friendly, drop-dead gorgeous, and not of the cloth. I was totally infatuated with her.

When I got into my bed, they came armed with all sorts of paraphernalia – a jug to pee in, a blood pressure machine, and all manner of other nurse stuff. Shortly thereafter, things started getting a little crazy. They closed the curtain around my bed, isolating me from the rest of the inmates. Doctors came and left. My bed was propped up and I was given some great drugs that completely relaxed me.

Before the drugs kicked in I had to make peace with Nurse Sally who had a face like thunder, "Hey Nurse Sally, I'm sorry…I just didn't…" and she turned on me, her piercing eyes bright with fury. "You just didn't think Paul…" she snapped, then her face softened "You just don't get it, do you? You're killing yourself…"

The next few weeks were kinda' weird. Twice I visited the Operating Room – things weren't looking so good. I even got last rites for the first time, appropriately from Father Nixon; a very Catholic experience meant to ease the way from this world to the next, I guess.

Then, one Sunday afternoon, a middle-aged lady showed up and introduced herself to me, "Hi Paul, I'm Anne Lander, do you mind if I sit down for a while and we can chat?"

She mentioned that Mum had asked her to come and visit me. Anne was well dressed and exuded an overwhelming sense of peace and serenity.

"Sure, please sit down and join me."

We chatted for a while; it was a fairly superficial conversation at first. We talked about the food and some of the people we both knew. Then the conversation got more intimate and it turned to God stuff. I wasn't all that wild about God at the time, so looking back, I'm pretty sure that it was deeply instilled manners coupled with fear of Mum's wrath that kept me from telling Anne to go to hell when she asked me if I minded if she prayed with me. She assured me that I didn't have to join in if I didn't want to and promised me that she wasn't about to get all weird with me.

She prayed for a little while and I let my guard down a bit.

Anne asked if I would mind if she laid her hands over where it hurt. "Sure," I said as I rolled over while she gently laid her soft hands on my lower back.

I could feel her relaxing. Then, I began to feel this incredible sensation from deep within me. It started as a dull pulse building in intensity until it throbbed before being replaced by an incredibly intense feeling of warmth and indescribable peace. I lay there; she sat there... neither of us moving for quite a while. Then it ended. I rolled over to look at Anne. I had no idea what had just happened, but at the same time, I knew that whatever it was, it was a significant event in my life. Anne looked drained, except for her eyes; they were alive and well, dancing with gaiety and love. She told me she'd be back in a couple of days, then she rose and lingered at the foot of my bed. "God bless you, Paul," she whispered, just loud enough for me to hear.

Soon after Anne left, it was time for afternoon rounds. When I peed into the jug, something I did at least twice a day every day, instead of the usual blood red specimen, it was as clear as pilsner beer. My blood pressure, instead of being ridiculously high, was normal. My sense of pain and discomfort was gone. Somewhat surprisingly, this seemed to confound some of the hospital folk far more than my antics had.

I ended up going to a hospital in England, Guys Clinic, where the answer was the same one we received back home. "I don't know what to tell you, but your medical records and what we see here do not really match. Good luck!"

The doctors preached caution. Their prescription for life – don't eat salt, don't drink alcohol, don't exercise vigorously, don't ride a motorcycle, don't drive on bumpy roads … the list went on and on and on. I saw Anne a few more times. At my last visit, her advice was, "Paul, no one knows how long you have. Make the most of it. Live your life to the full."

As I left that final afternoon, standing in the doorway, I turned to look at her one last time and she whispered, "God bless you, Paul."

So I went back to my life at school and did all the things that teenage boys do. Went to bars, got drunk, chased girls, played sports, and studied just enough to pass my exams. On the academic front, English Literature was my passion and I was fortunate enough to be taught by a man who had the ability to bring any prose to life. He was straightforward and told it like it was. One day, he stood in front of the class and said, "If you want to come to my class, do. If you want to do the homework I set, do. It is entirely up to you."

I never missed a class nor handed a paper in late. Chaucer, Shakespeare, Hemingway and Wilfred Owen became my erstwhile friends. I competed in swimming, water polo, rugby, and track and field with varying degrees of success. Life was good. Life was really good.

I was incredibly fortunate to finish my school career as a member of a squad that went on a Rugby tour to England. We had a relatively successful tour and a great time. After the tour, a few of us decided to stay in England and use it as a base from which we'd explore the rest of the world.

Chapter 2

Living on My Terms

Overseas
December, 1986

I spent Christmas with my family in a little village in the south of England called Westcott where Mum's brother Tim and his family lived.

New Years Eve arrived and I left the sleepy little village to meet up with my mates in London where we spent the evening carousing with hundreds of thousands of other revelers. We spent a fun filled evening bar-hopping, sight-seeing and people-watching. For a group of incredibly naïve little eighteen-year-old boys from Africa, the sights of punks sporting mohawks and girls in sexy outfits were as intoxicating as the beer we drank. We got ripped off in Soho, the infamous red light district, by a fairly rough looking overweight tart in a cat suit, who after taking our cash, drunkenly staggered around the stage to some out of date show tunes. Just before midnight, we moved on to join everyone else at Trafalgar Square to welcome in the New Year.

The countdown began, "Ten, nine, eight" … This was it! 1987 was to be the year that I would travel the globe and discover the meaning of life, or at the very least, drink lots of beer and meet hot women …"seven, six, five" … I wondered what the year ahead held for this naïve, rather immature adventurer …"four, three, two" … Wow, there are more people here than I've ever seen before and that girl's pretty cute …"One! Happy New Year!"

Over a hundred thousand voices chorused. The cute girl and I kept eye contact as, all around us, people hugged and kissed. As the first few chords of "Auld Lang Syne" rang out, I worked my way over to the cute girl and she kissed me. "Happy New Year, I'm Liz." Raging hormones fueled by a few too many beers gave me the courage to ask Liz for her phone number and for some reason she gave it to me. Oh yes, 1987 was going to be a great year.

Having started really well, the year continued that way. A couple of days after meeting Liz, Mum married a chap named Stewart. The two of them had been friends for a few years and he deserved a medal for sticking around as I hadn't made things easy for either of them. It didn't take a shrink to figure out that I was just a jealous, over protective, insecure teenager trying to look after my own interests.

Fortunately, Mum and Stewart handled me well and they've gone on over the years to make each other happy. They are right together in much the same way that my dad and his wife Margi are right together.

Mum and Stewart's wedding was awesome. Joined by family and friends, Mum looked lovely in her ruby silk dress and the groom, dapper in his suit. The reception was held at a quaint little hotel in the country and a fine time was had by all. A few days later, Lisa and the newlyweds returned home to Zimbabwe and I set off to discover what life had to offer.

To start with, I shared a room with Anton, a dear friend of mine from Zimbabwe. We lived in Mrs. Bell's boarding house in Kilburn, North London. It was a lot of fun. She rented rooms, mostly to young foreigners. Some of the folk who'd lived there for a while showed us the ropes. There were only a few rules, and cardinal amongst them was that there was to be no shagging. After spending a couple of days exploring the area and checking out the pubs, I became a little despondent on the employment front as there didn't seem to be any organizations recruiting eighteen-year-old foreigners with no work experience to come in and run the show.

I decided to give Liz, of Trafalgar Square fame, a call. To my surprise, not only did she take my call, she also agreed to meet me for a beer that night after she finished work. We met at a pub on Oxford Street named "Hog in the Pound", and she was great. She was easy to talk to and fun to be with. We parted ways that night with a brief kiss. As she walked away down Oxford Street, her firm derriere swinging from side to side, the frustrated virgin inside me groaned.

Later that night, Anton and I discussed my predicament. Here was this beautiful girl, who actually seemed to like me, and I had no idea what to do next. We came up with a plan. Leafing through my wallet past the two dog-eared condoms that had been hidden there for the past few years, I pulled out her phone number, and then did what any horny bloke would do. I called her up and invited her to join me for dinner.

We arranged to meet back at the same pub at seven o'clock the following evening. Though it was the middle of winter, beads of nervous sweat dripped down my spine as I rode the underground tube into town that night. I got there early with plenty of time to spare. I got a table, and as I waited, I had a few drinks and tried ever so hard to look cool.

Liz was as wonderful as I'd imagined she'd be. She took my breath away when she let her overcoat slip from her shoulders before sitting down next to me. I'd never met anyone like her before, or anyone who dressed the way she did. That night, she was wearing an immaculately tailored cream business suit. She had the musky scent of a sensuous woman and expensive perfume. Dinner was a blur. We chatted about everything and nothing at the same time. As the meal wore on, the atmosphere got more and more sexually charged when I asked Liz if she'd like to finish off the meal with a cup of coffee. She looked me square in the eyes, hers glinting like a lioness moving in for the kill and her hand lightly caressing my thigh. "Sure," she purred, "but let's have it at your place."

Oh my. I left enough money on the table to cover the tab plus a generous tip and eagerly led Liz to catch the very next train to Kilburn. The ride home was exquisite hell filled with forbidden promise. I briefed Liz on the way that Mrs. Bell had certain rules, so we'd need to sneak into the house and then she'd have to wait for me in my bedroom whilst I went downstairs to the kitchen to make some coffee. She was a really good sport. In fact, she was pretty amused with the whole setup. After ensuring that all was clear, we snuck up to my room. I asked her to make herself comfortable before reluctantly dashing downstairs to make some coffee.

Sneaking back upstairs, I slid into the room. "Do you have milk and sug …" I began to ask before the words died abruptly in my throat. I put the tray down and just stared at Liz. I must have looked like a bunny in the headlights to her. There she was, my fantasy brought to life. Her athletically chiseled porcelain body, her finely manicured painted scarlet nails, her recently released trusses of golden hair, and her ivory stockings held up by garters with the skimpiest panties that matched her sexy bra. I also noticed that she was wearing nothing else. She came to me. We kissed. We kissed some more. "I've never done anything like this …" "Don't worry" she assured me "I have …" It was an incredible night.

Liz and I saw each other a few more times before I set off on my first journey down the destructive path that ruined every significant relationship that I'd have with a woman. Here was Liz, a girl who I adored and who liked me too, but wasn't enough to keep me around.

Reading through a travel magazine on one cold winter Monday morning, I spied an advert beckoning me to come and work on a moshav in Israel. A moshav is a cooperative community of farmers. A few hours later, I was at the Israeli embassy sorting out a visa. That Thursday night, I was strapped into my seat as the jumbo jet screamed down the runway bound for Tel Aviv. Before we got airborne, part of the engine fell off, and we were delayed for awhile. This was not altogether a bad thing as the flight was mostly filled with other kibbutz and moshav volunteers. Many of us made our way to the bar, partly to celebrate the fact that we were still alive, and partly to gain some false courage before having to climb into an airplane again.

Before I got hammered, my conscience got the better of me, and I called Liz to tell her that I was leaving. We fought and argued for awhile. The only things we seemed to agree on were that she wasn't happy and that I was a complete shit. The worst part of the call for me was when she asked me why I was doing this and why I'd handled it the way that I did. I couldn't give her an answer because I didn't have one, which disappointed, saddened and insulted her. Truthfully, it scared and saddened me, too. I knew that I adored almost everything about her, but at the same time, every ounce of my being was screaming at me to get the hell out of there, and to run.

Waking up in Tel Aviv as the plane touched down, even the low-grade hangover and high-grade sense of guilt couldn't subdue my excitement. There was a heady scent in the air, a blend of unfamiliar flowers mixed with dust and body odor. Brand new to me, it was at the same time strangely familiar. In fact, the more I looked around, the more I was confronted with the familiarity of my youth in Rhodesia. I recognized it in the mood of the Israeli people. Most of the young ones were toting guns and dressed in camouflage. There was nothing unusual about this to any of them. It was the familiarity and the camaraderie that I recognized from my youth and through recognizing it, I recognized how much I missed it.

In Tel Aviv, I noticed that the people walked with purpose. They laughed from deep within, all too aware that this laugh could be their last. They lounged in chairs outside cosmopolitan coffee shops. The accents were Israeli, American, English, French, Australian and South African. The languages were English, Albanian, Yiddish, Japanese, Spanish and Afrikaans. It was intoxicating when all of the different voices came together. Their tone and cadence left you with no doubt that everyone knew and accepted that death might be just around the corner, but to hell with all of that. Today was a good day to be alive. I was in my element.

A few days after arriving in Israel I boarded a bus and set off to whatever was next. After feasting on cold Coke and warm falafels at the bus terminal, I spent the next few hours in awe as we drove out into the country. After leaving the coast, we soon found ourselves in the middle of some of the most rugged terrain I've ever come across. Jagged peaks littered with hardcore scrub blended with miles and miles of barren desert and an occasional veritable oasis the locals called moshav. I was blown away at the vision, ingenuity and determination of the Israelis who'd built towns and farms where camels would have feared to tread.

The driver stopped the bus in the middle of nowhere and told me that it was time for me and my backpack to get off. More than a little anxious about getting dropped off all alone in the middle of the Negev Desert, the bus driver cheerily assured me that someone would be along soon to take me the rest of the way to my moshav. Watching the bus's taillights disappear in the distance, I took stock of my situation; I wondered if I should be nervous about being so close to the Jordanian border, which was only a few miles away. To the west rose the Negev Mountains, and to the east, the mountains of Edom. It all felt very biblical.

As I sat there waiting, I wondered what I'd gotten myself into before my thoughts were thankfully interrupted by the rumble of a diesel tractor as its high beam headlights pierced the lunar nightscape. With very little ceremony, I was picked up and taken to a house that I would share with a couple of totally out of control English chaps.

Over the course of a few cold beers, my new life was explained to me. At that point, I still wasn't all that sure what a moshav was. The short version is that back in the 1980's a moshav was a group of families who brought in people like me, mostly youngsters from The Americas, Europe, Austral-Asia and southern Africa to be cheap farm labor. It seemed like a great trade to me. In return for our services, we got to work in the fields in the Holy Land. Many of us were fleeing the frigid Northern Hemisphere winter and escaping to a paradise where, as a moshavnik, you could get a great suntan, make some friends, collect a barrel full of great memories and find loads of opportunities to party your arse off. There I was, one of a couple hundred "kids" who'd gathered from around the world to work in the fields and pack sheds by day, and drink beer and party at night. It was awesome.

As for the moshav I was working on, its claim to fame is that all sorts of fruits and vegetables, herbs and spices are grown there; tomatoes, peppers, zucchinis, melons, watermelons, mangoes and dates are just some of the produce grown in this manmade oasis. Some of the produce is sold locally while the rest is exported. My job was to pick tomatoes.

I'd get picked up by our farmer's son at the break of day and then try to get as much work done before it got too hot to work. I made my way up and down the lines of tomato bushes, hunchbacked as I picked the ripe tomatoes. The brutal desert sun would quickly burn away any remnants of the previous night's excesses. At midday, I'd get out of the sun. It was siesta time. I'd eat, sleep, read or do whatever I felt like before returning to the fields for a few more hours of picking tomatoes which brought me to the end of an honest day's work. Having worked hard, it was time to play hard.

Israel was a lot of fun. Too much fun for me as it turned out. I was a little too immature, drank a little too much, and partied a little too hard. Not a good combination. Pini, the Israeli chap who I worked with, tried to save me from myself. It was quite something since I know he thought I was an arse. I remember early on when I was complaining about the blisters on my hands, he grabbed a hold of them, stared at them for a while, and then contemptuously and accurately pronounced that I'd never done a hard day's work in my life.

Letting my hands drop, Pini went on to tell me all about how his family had come to Israel to build their future. He spoke of the hardship and the persecution his people had suffered. He told of his time in the army, how as a young man, barely more than a boy, he'd fought in the Six Day War. He was very grateful he had lived when so many others hadn't.

Pini was a proud, fair man, and fortunately for me, he was the one who got to decide my fate late one particularly drunken night. I got it in my head to load up the tractor and trailer with wine and women and head off to party by a fire that burned on the mountainside across the border in Jordan. With my common sense dulled by whiskey and beer, and oblivious to the risk of being blown up by landmines, I was bound and determined to have my good time. Fortunately, none of us got hurt or killed before we were caught and stopped. As the driver of the tractor and the mastermind behind the ill-conceived foray, I received an expedited flight back to the cold and gray of London, England.

The reception I received in England made me wish that I'd been shot or blown up by either the Israelis or Jordanians. With the exception of my sister Lisa and my cousins Helen and Pal, my family was pissed. My uncle Tim, a great bloke, was beginning to see that there may have been a little more to "keeping an eye on me" than he'd bargained for when he'd made the commitment to Mum.

Undaunted by the task, he took me up to the local pub; as we drank our beers, we made peace and came up with a plan. My penance was that I'd go and spend the next few months working for a friend of a friend down in the country. I agreed to commit to at least three months down there as it was felt by the grown-ups that that would be the least amount of time that I'd need to see the error of my ways. Everyone seemed to agree that the fresh country air and a little hard labor would do me a world of good.

So I went to work for a timber company. I lived with my boss Simon and his wife Susan. During the first month, there were times when I thought that I'd died and gone to hell as I staggered on the brink of exhaustion. We'd be in the forests from before the sun came up and we wouldn't leave until it went down again. My days were filled with lugging gear, swinging chainsaws and my specialty, gathering all the crap into piles so that it could be burned.

I was under no illusions as to where I stood. I was at the bottom of the food chain. My job was to work hard and keep my mouth shut. At the end of each day, I'd have dinner with Simon and Susan. Then, I'd roll into bed and sleep the sleep of the dead. The only thing I didn't consider doing was quitting, and that was only because my uncle Tim had done a number on me. As we sat in the pub waiting for the train to come and take me away, he said to me, "It's going to be tough," he said, "but you'll get through it. Remember though, if you quit, you'll know that you quit forever."

So I didn't quit. I played the game. Simon and Susan were great to me. They were a young couple who lived life the right way. They just seemed to have a knack for doing the next right thing; they gave me the time and the space to figure things out. When the three months were over, we parted ways. Simon didn't need the extra hand anymore and I was itching to get back to London to pick up where I'd left off, with wine, women and song. That was all I was after.

Lee – Life as a Lifeguard

I got a job as a lifeguard at a swimming pool in central London. I thought that I'd hit the jackpot; I'd get paid to lounge around and admire girls in their skimpy bathing suits all day long. Well, that turned out to be a very small part of my workday; the mundane predictability of the job bored me to tears as I walked around the pool, time and time again. I couldn't wait to get out of the building at the end of each shift and race to meet up with Lee, an American lass who'd stolen my heart. We strolled hand in hand through the streets of London, and swam in the ocean off the beaches in Crete. We lived, loved, and laughed our way through an unforgettable summer.

Unfortunately, it all ended in tears as I once again waited until things were going really well and then screwed it up. The details seem pretty irrelevant today; there was someone else, there was a lot of beer, I was selfish and I ran away. The only relevance is that I hurt someone I loved and had created a behavior pattern that was going to follow me for many years to come.

I toiled purely to make money so that I could travel the globe. I picked up odd jobs along the way. Sometimes I'd work as a barman or as a waiter. Sometimes, I'd pick up work as a building laborer. I liked it when I could mix cement and carry bricks, as that paid more. I spent some time with a group of friends, traveling around, putting up marquee tents, and once, I even took part in a drug trial. I got to see some of the world and meet some incredible people along the way.

I gleefully took part in all-night binges and savored exotic food and company whenever I could. I leapt into conversations, some of which are still going strong today. I lusted after some exceptional women and slept very little. I thought life was good, but it was spiraling out of control. The only thing I knew for sure was that I was pushing myself toward a big fall.

Army Time

I laid in my seat onboard the PanAm flight that took me back to England after a rip-roaring visit to America. I had saved up some money and, with a friend of mine, took a trip to visit his father who owned a restaurant in Aspen, Colorado. The visit included some fantastic skiing, and some even better après ski, especially for a nineteen-year-old. A lucky spell in Las Vegas had led to an even luckier spell in an awesome little coastal college town in California. It was fun living on the edge, answering to no one, going where I wanted, when I wanted, and doing what I wanted with whom I wanted. At least that's what I told myself. The truth was that it was beginning to get old and quite frankly, lonely. In the instances when I was honest with myself I'd acknowledge that I was starting to crave some structure in my life. I wanted to be accountable to someone, to be responsible for something more than getting wasted and trying to get laid.

Given my family's military background, I always assumed that I'd spend some time in uniform. Weaned on tales and images of my family's military exploits, I decided that the time had come to just do it. The day after my flight landed from America, clean and fresh and glowing, dressed in fresh khakis, a pressed white oxford shirt, paisley tie and tweed sports coat, I made my way down to Trafalgar Square. I strode purposely through the drizzle past Nelson's Column, managing to avoid both the puddles and the bird poop as I headed towards the Army recruiting office.

The night before, I'd sat in a pub and over the course of a few beers and a few shots of Benedictine, I chain-smoked my way through the decision process. "What am I doing? Why am I doing this?" I asked myself over and over. The answer was both simple and clear to me – it had always been in the cards, my life was spiraling out of control, and it seemed like the thing to do. Besides, it was only for a few years on a Short Service Commission. I wasn't talking about soldiering for the rest of my life.

Once inside the recruiting office, I met up with the recruiting officer at the appointed hour and I learned all I needed to know. After signing a few forms, I began the process of enlisting into Her Majesty's Forces.

After filling out loads of paperwork, passing numerous interviews, and doing everything that needed to be done, the day finally arrived. Standing on my own in a nondescript Ministry of Defense office, I swore an oath of allegiance to Queen and country and was enlisted into the Army. My recruiting officer shook my hand, and then gave me a piece of paper with a date, an address, and all the information I needed in order to report for basic training. I was classified as a P.O., a Potential Officer.

As I was not British, but rather someone from the Commonwealth, if I wanted to be an officer, I needed to complete basic training and serve with the troops before my officer training could begin. I was to report to Woolwich Arsenal to train with the Royal Artillery before moving on to my chosen regiment, the Army Air Corps.

A glitch in the process meant that I had a couple of weeks before I had to report for duty so I needed to figure out what to do in the meantime. It was an easy decision, as Maria was now in my life. Maria was exquisite, feisty, and filled with an incredible sense of daring and adventure. Being in her presence was intoxicating. The only problem was that she was in Michigan in America, and I was in London, England. I really wanted to see her before I fell off the face of the earth and entered the green machine.

We had a lot of open questions, not least of which was whether or not we had a future together. I did a pre-enlistment whirlwind tour of Michigan, which really didn't go so well. I arrived on the train platform at Woolwich Arsenal on my way to report for duty with a broken heart as I hobbled along on crutches. The broken heart was the result of a relationship that was over. The crutches resulted from a poorly executed snowboarding maneuver.

I crutched my way to the group of shaking civilians who were being hollered at by a bunch of ranting individuals dressed in army uniforms. I went up to the chap who looked as if he were in charge. Once he stopped screaming long enough to take a breath, I asked him in my clipped accent, "Excuse me sir, I'm here to report for basic training. Would you be so kind as to tell me where to go? Templer's the name."

His face went puce. "First off, you see these stripes on my arm? I work for a living!" He ranted. "You will call me Bombardier and only when I speak to you! Secondly, what the hell are you doing here on crutches?"

Taken aback and more than a little frightened, I held out my papers and told him that I'd messed up my Achilles tendon and that I was supposed to be here at this time on this day.

A couple of hours and numerous rants later, I was back on the train platform. In my Army Envelope, I now had medical papers and a new "report to hell" date. Looking at the upside, I figured when I returned to Woolwich without my crutches I'd be far better prepared for what lay ahead, or so I thought.

About six weeks into training, I remember standing at attention in eager anticipation for the weekend that lay ahead. My fellow gunners and I had our heads shaved, our bodies toned, and our boots shined. This was the first significant milestone on our road to becoming soldiers. We were Martinique Troop, fitness troop, and we were damned proud of it. Whilst others specialize in drill or other soldier-like pursuits, we ran and worked out till we dry heaved and then we ran some more. We hated it but we loved it. We worked hard and now with our first weekend pass, it was time to go and play hard.

This whole soldiering thing was turning out to be okay. I'd been plagued by injuries but was thankfully still with my troop. The mental games were a little tougher. I accepted that the instructors were there to mess with us. I knew that they needed to break us down before they could build us back up. At an academic level, I knew that it was all part of the process. I couldn't always understand why some of our instructors did some of the things they did, but given my background, growing up surrounded by the military, I gave them the benefit of the doubt and tried to accept that there was method to their madness. I really respected most of my instructors, though they drove us pretty hard. I knew that one day, when I was caught up in the middle of it, with bullets whizzing by and bombs exploding, I would do my job properly; and along with my comrades in arms, I might live to tell the tale.

There was, however, one instructor who seemed to be particularly committed to breaking us down, presumably so that he could build us back up. He'd get us out of bed in the middle of the night, and mess with us. We were on the third floor of the barrack block, and he'd have us scrambling to attention, and then he would stumble around the room, destroying hours of work that we had spent ironing, shining and polishing equipment.

As we stood there at attention willing our weekend to begin, he strode up towards us screaming "You fuckers make me sick. You disgust me and embarrass me. You obviously don't know what to do with your equipment so I'm going to show you. Now, go upstairs and put your combat gear on over the uniform that you're wearing now. Weekend passes are cancelled. You have two minutes."

As we sprinted up six flights of stairs, none of us had any idea what he was talking about. Our Commanding Officer had just released us off the square. We all thought that we'd done well and surely that meant that we were good to go.

That was the beginning of the end of my military career. Our battery had spent weeks bonding during basic training. We learned to work together as a team, and on that team, we developed different roles – some official, others unofficial. There were the obvious natural born leaders and then there were those who were more comfortable following. There were those who were strong and then there were those who were getting stronger.

Among this group of individuals, there was one guy who stood out as the strongest, and we called him Scouse. Scouse was born and bred in Liverpool. As a Paratrooper, he'd gone through the notorious "P Company", the British Army Paratrooper selection and training course. Scouse was pure paratrooper – strong, brave, and loyal to a fault. He led by example and could often be found helping the stragglers along when need be. Unfortunately, Scouse had recently developed a respiratory infection, but due to his exquisite conditioning, he had managed to stay the course and "Pass off the Square".

We went up and down the stairs over and over again, each time adding a new layer of clothing. It was the middle of summer. It had to be ninety degrees in the shade with as much humidity as the air could handle.

We were all suffering and Scouse was suffering the most. We'd just put on yet another layer and I could see that his breathing was becoming erratic as his eyes bulged. He wasn't complaining, he wouldn't, but it was clear to all of us that he couldn't take much more of this abuse. I tried reasoning with the Bombardier again to let Scouse be. He ridiculed me, and punished the rest of the lads because I'd dared to speak without being spoken to. He made them do pushups and made me stand there watching.

Our NBC (Nuclear Biological Chemical) kit with respirators was the next call. We trudged up the stairs, bent double, the sweat-soaked layers of kit stuck to our exhausted bodies. A couple of us helped Scouse put on his NBC suit, which was particularly cumbersome. It was a charcoal filled, army green outfit. It was designed to help soldiers survive nuclear, biological or chemical weapons, for a while. When it came time for us to put on his respirator, I felt Scouse's skin. It was cool and dry and as he tried unsuccessfully to put on his helmet, I could see that his coordination was totally shot. Half dragging, half carrying him, we stumbled past the Bombardier who, while smirking, hoofed a well-placed polished boot up my arse. I lost it and went bezerk and probably would have killed him and thrown him over the balcony had I not been restrained.

Hearing all the commotion, some of the other instructors joined the fracas, called the men to attention and then gave us all leave to go and enjoy our weekend pass. Before I left, I was called before my instructors and given a severe bollocking. It wasn't nearly as severe as the one I expected or deserved, but it was there all the same and the incident would stain my record. It was not the best way to start a military career. The rest of basic training went by in a blur. I was grateful for the opportunity to captain our troop to victory in our intakes Rugby tournament, and was later asked to play for the regiment. My Passing Out Parade was one of the proudest days of my life as it signified my evolution from civilian, to recruit, to soldier. I was very proud to be a part of such a professional organization.

The highlight of my Army career followed when I was attached to 658 Squadron Army Air Corps which was part of the 5th Airborne

Brigade, a fighting unit which was the heart of Britain's rapid intervention capability that lead NATO's rapid reaction force in the 1990's. I played rugby for the squadron, got to do some soldiering and generally reveled in the experiences and the camaraderie.

The future looked bright until I had a problem with my aviation medical. We discovered that I was susceptible to hay fever. I would not be able to become a helicopter pilot. Shortly thereafter, I had a chat with my Squadron Sergeant Major. He was a great chap, a man who I respected immensely. He told me that I probably wasn't going to get to follow the path I'd planned for my military career, but he stressed that it wasn't the end of the road. There were other options and other regiments to serve in that would suit me well.

Considering my Squadron Sergeant Major's counsel, I completed my attachment and continued serving in the Army for a while longer. As I did so, my mind kept going back to a night I'd spent on a training exercise. The damp had long ago worked its way into my bones as I hunched over, turning away from the cold wind, my hand shaking ever so slightly as I hugged my rifle. My mouth was dry and my body reacted to the huge jolts of adrenaline coursing through it. My body and mind had truly been pushed to their limits.

I lay there in wait with my comrades in arms; one was a former Legionnaire in the French Foreign Legion, another served in the Special Air Service, and the third was an Irishman martial artist extraordinaire who'd spent some time with the Royal Marines. I'd realized that I was the odd man out. Though I could soldier with the very best of them, they were soldiers.

A few months later, once it became obvious I could not become a helicopter pilot, and having considered the many options that I was extremely grateful were presented to me, I chose to leave the Army and was granted an Honorable Discharge with an Exemplary Conduct. As curious as it was to me that this was offered, I accepted it, and by doing so, accepted that I would not follow in the footsteps of my military forefathers.

With an Honorable Discharge from Her Majesty's Forces, I moved on with my life. Looking back at those days, they were some of the proudest of my life. I was blessed to meet and serve with some of the finest people I'm sure that I'll ever come across. I'll always have the utmost respect for the men and women of the British Military.

Post-Amy Overseas

Waking up the morning after I'd left the Army was not a pleasant experience. I opened one eye ever so slowly and when that didn't seem like such a good idea, I let it drop shut again. In that brief second, I had caught a glimpse of my sister Lisa's worried face as it swam in and out of focus. My head throbbed, my queasy stomach heaved and my mouth tasted terrible. I drank way too much the night before. I didn't remember getting back to my sister's semi-detached north London house, but I knew that the night before had been rough as I was curled up in a mucky heap at the foot of the stairs.

I spent my first few days as a civilian responding to job ads in the newspapers and going for interviews through employment agencies, but soon realized that being out of the Army had seemed far better as an idea, than as reality. I wasn't quite ready to throw in the towel and return to the Army just yet. I thought I'd have some fun first. I decided to go back to a formula that I knew worked for me. I gave up looking for a career. All I needed was some money to travel.

After considering my strengths, there was one thing that I knew I did really well and that was fighting. I figured I could either be an underground prize fighter or a bouncer. I soon found a job as a bouncer at a fairly dodgy club in north London.

Things went pretty smoothly during my first night on the job. That was right up until about three o'clock in the morning when I received a

"Code Red", which was nightclub lingo for "the shit is hitting the fan." Sean, a huge Greek guy with dark curly hair who was way too nice to do this job for long, was showing me the ropes. He and I hustled as quickly as we could towards the designated area.

We were met by a bloody mass that five minutes earlier had been a walking, talking person. He was now propped up on a table, staring lifelessly at the dirty ceiling. He was bleeding from his head. Blood was splattered all over his torn white dress shirt which was still tucked into his expensive looking charcoal pants held up by a slim black dress belt. There was even blood on his blue socks and black slip-on shoes.

It turned out that the local Chinese and Turkish gangs were in the middle of a turf war and our merry little establishment soon became the setting for way too many confrontations. This Turkish guy had made the mistake of getting drunk and wandering off from the rest of his gang. Spotting an easy target, a few of the Chinese chaps grabbed hold of him and held him down while one of them tried to reshape his skull with a snooker ball.

The pool of blood, dim lights, smoky haze, and the victim's disjointed movements made the whole experience a little weird. What was even weirder was that no one else seemed to give a damn. I wanted to call an ambulance or the cops, but no. This was to be handled by the gang members themselves. The victim's mates manhandled the barely breathing lump of meat down the stairs. The Chinese racked up the balls, smoked cigarettes, and got on with whatever the hell they were doing at four in the morning.

And so began a fascinating few months where I got to live in this strange new parallel universe. I realized that not only was there money to be made after dark, but that there was a whole other world out there. A world that until then, I'd only imagined existed. It was a world populated by gangs, cops, drunks, pimps, porno actresses, artists, bums and lost souls looking for the meaning of life. I had an absolute ball.

Then I met Meg, a beautiful girl on her way to Hong Kong to work for a few months as an aerobics and aquarobics instructor. It wasn't just her beauty that attracted me. She had a quick smile, razor wit, and deep down, she was a good person. I fell for her and she seemed to fall for me, too. We liked each other enough that we planned to meet up in India once she finished her contract in Hong Kong. We were going to travel around India in style. We planned to see the country from the comfort of a five star steam train as we followed the paths of the Maharajas. Then, we would lounge on the beaches in Goa, take it one day at a time, and see what might happen.

India

Whilst Meg was in Hong Kong, I managed to keep myself out of trouble. I found a job as a security guard with a private security company and was contracted to News International. The work was as uneventful as work could possibly be. The only excitement was on the rare occasion when one of the journalists would write an article that would irritate some unstable soul who'd feel obligated to express his frustration to the journalist concerned. This was seldom done in a controlled, constructive or positive manner. This didn't happen anywhere nearly as often as you'd think it should and slowly but surely, days turned into weeks, weeks turned into months and before I knew it, it was time for me to go to India.

As I stepped out of the airplane and into the boiling sunshine, my smile was abruptly wiped off my face as I was overwhelmed by the unmistakably rotten smell of death that fought with the taste and scent of squalor rising above the shantytown that was much of Bombay. I gagged and just managed to stop myself from vomiting as I stumbled backwards. I caught hold of the handrail, which saved me from tumbling down the steps. I've smelt dead bodies before, but nothing could have prepared me for the smell of that place.

I tried to put the smell into perspective as I called to mind the fact that I'd be meeting up with Meg the next day. I had to admit that when we planned this trip while lounging in the park in London, basking in the sunshine and sipping on glasses of red wine, it seemed a lot more romantic than when I stepped off the plane. Not to be put off, I pulled myself together, looked back over my shoulder, smiled, and bid the beautiful flight attendant adieu. I then made my way through customs and immigration and on to my hotel.

The Sea and Sands Hotel was nestled next to a Sheraton. It was exactly what I was after when I'd booked the room; clean, incredibly comfortable, and it felt like the right place to start our adventure. That night I readied myself for Meg's arrival; I ordered the champagne and the ice bucket. I chatted to the florist and selected the flowers. I checked to make sure that her flight was scheduled to arrive on time and then ordered a cab that would get me there with plenty of time to spare, just in case her flight got in early.

I was giddy with anticipation as I stood there clutching one dozen long-stemmed red roses, waiting for Meg to walk through from the Arrivals hall and back into my life. As more and more of the passengers from her Cathay Pacific flight made their way through, my heady anticipation turned into a sense of dread. I tried unsuccessfully to get some information from the incredibly rude and unhelpful chap with the airline. It was over an hour since the first few passengers had arrived. The stream of people who'd followed them had slowed to a trickle and then finally an incredibly pissed off Aussie couple stalked through and assured me that they were the very last ones off the flight.

I went back to the airline desk to ask the rep for help and I may have imagined a smirk. Whether or not it actually happened is irrelevant; to me, he smirked. The smug, self-satisfied bastard had, in his ever so perfect Queen's English, strung me along all afternoon as he'd sat playing with his computer, every so often glancing at me with his bitter eyes. He had an officious air about him. He came across as someone who resented his lot in life, who as a victim of his circumstances, was going to be as big a pain in the arse as a flesh-encapsulated organism possibly could.

To his credit though, his finely tuned people skills coupled with his ability to read the evolving situation saved us both a lot of trouble as he accurately read the rage on my face along with my intent to inflict grievous bodily harm upon him. I leapt over the counter, determined to get some information out of him one way or another, but right before I got to him, he blurted out in not so perfect high-pitched Indian English. "She cancelled her flight two weeks ago ..."

Had I been shot with an elephant gun, it wouldn't have stunned me more than those seven little words. I stopped and just stood there awhile. Unsure of what to do next, I thanked him for the information, and then, leaving my long-stemmed red roses on the counter, I walked out to the diminished taxi rank, hailed a cab and made my way back to my hotel, alone. There I went to the bar and proceeded to get very, very drunk and then as the evening wore on, I got very, very stupid.

Before getting to India, I'd been warned about what to eat and drink and what to avoid. "Don't drink the water. Don't even eat the salad; it's probably been rinsed in the water. Don't have ice in your drinks, again because of the water, and be careful that what you eat has been well cooked." As the night wore on, I dismissed those warnings as whining protests from weak, unadventurous souls. I continued to sip my scotch on the rocks, and ordered Steak Tartare and Lobster Thermidor.

Early the following morning, I was jolted awake with a stomach spasm so intense I cried out into my empty room. Stumbling, I made it to the loo just in time as I immediately vomited into the sink. "Bombay Belly" had claimed me as her next victim. Scenes from the previous morning when I'd watched the carts rolling through the shantytown being loaded up with the dead didn't seem so surreal anymore as wave after wave of nausea rolled over me and spasm after spasm wracked my body. Hours later I woke up again, drenched in sweat and who knows what else. I was totally spent as I lay there, curled around the toilet bowl. I felt awful and being somewhat melodramatic, I thought for sure that I was going to die.

Seeking some comfort and support, I called my sister Lisa in England. She wasn't there, so instead, I spoke to my best friend in the world, her husband Rory. He found my predicament incredibly amusing. "Let me get this right, you traveled half-way 'round the world to meet this girl. She stood you up. You have a case of the screaming shits and you can't get a flight out of there for a few more days … that's funnier 'n hell."

Having lost a lot of weight, I arrived back in England. After laying low for a while, I started thinking about what was going to happen next. As far as Meg was concerned, I found out through the letter she sent me (that arrived the day I left for India) that she'd met some bloke in Thailand on her way to India and they'd gotten waylaid. Meg and I have seen each other since and we're great friends now that my belly, my heart, and my ego have fully recovered.

I was done with love for a while and was seriously considering rejoining the Army. I'd met with a couple of regiments and was getting close to returning when Mum and Lisa intervened by way of giving me a ticket home to Zimbabwe for Christmas. The idea was that I could take a break from making bad decisions, clear my mind, get rid of the lingering stomach bug that had stayed with me since India, and then just take some time to gain perspective on my life.

At the time, it was one of the best things that could have happened to me. I was subjected to my family's tender loving care, healthy home cooked meals, a monster course of antibiotics, the chance to catch up on a lot of sleep and plenty of time to think. I was soon feeling stronger physically, mentally and spiritually.

Part of my rehab included spending time out in the sun enjoying the great outdoors. As a Christmas present, Mum sent Lisa and I off to Victoria Falls to raft the mighty Zambezi River.

Chapter 3

Safari Adventures

Back Home
January 1991

A rriving in Victoria Falls, Lisa and I checked into our hotel. Not long after that, I made my way down to the pool, made myself comfortable on one of the deck chairs, ordered an ice cold beer and was thinking about how it was a lot hotter in Africa than I remembered. Then, Greg and Tracy, friends of Lisa who lived and worked in the "Falls", showed up. Greg was an expert river guide and was going to take us rafting.

The following day, Greg did a spectacular job guiding the self-bailing gray pig of a raft safely through the roaring, crashing, tumultuous white water. I was completely blown away by the experience. The preamble hadn't oversold it one little bit. It was great fun! I got to experience the adrenaline pumping, awe inspiring, almost religious experience on one of the most beautiful stretches of river in the world. It was pleasing to the eye and soothing to the soul. To make things even better, that night I got to party with Greg and his mates, a bunch of fellow river guides.

Reluctantly, Lisa and I left Victoria Falls and headed back to town to spend the last week or so of our holiday with Mum and Stewart. Back in town, I had to make a choice. I could go back to England to join the Army, I could work security in Angola, a euphemism for working as a mercenary, or I could accept an offer for a job in the safari industry. The question then was did I want to shoot people with guns or shoot wildlife with a camera? Did I want to kill people, or did I want to coexist with nature? I accepted the safari offer.

Safari Guide

"Fuck! Fuck! Fuck! Fuck!" Tears of rage mixed with the pouring rain flowed down my cheeks as I waved my Ruger Redhawk .44 magnum revolver around like a crazy man and bellowed like a gut-shot buffalo. I was aiming to shoot other people. As I searched in vain for my targets, a bolt of lightning lit up my world and revealed a tent peg embedded in my bare foot and the poachers getting away.

For almost a year now, I'd been working as a professional river guide on the lower Zambezi River. To me, the best way in the world to experience African wildlife is from the back of a Canadian style canoe.

The Zambezi is a magnificent river that changes by the day and by the mile. We'd pass through gorges, floodplains, wide water, and narrow channels, drifting slowly past herds of elephant and buffalo wallowing in the river. I watched crocodiles slither from sunny sandbanks before disappearing into who knows where? (At the time, the Department of National Parks estimated that there was one crocodile over six feet long for every forty yards of river frontage on the lower Zambezi River).

I got to observe lion, waterbuck, wild dog, impala, kudu, warthogs, baboons and all the other creatures living just the way nature intended. I glided nervously past pods of inquisitive hippo, which as a species, are responsible each year for killing more people than any other animal. All the while, I was surrounded by hundreds of different species of birds, bugs, and reptiles. A canoe safari on the Zambezi River has to be one of life's most incredible experiences.

In the tourism industry in Zimbabwe, we took the whole safari thing pretty seriously, and to get licensed as a safari guide of any description was a big deal. Anyone who is serious about working in the Safari industry starts off by getting their Learner Professional Hunter's license before going on to decide what their specialty is going to be. Some choose hunting while others choose to guide photographic safaris either on land or on the rivers.

To be a successful professional safari guide, whether guiding clients on land or in the water, whether shooting the wildlife with a camera or a gun, the aspiring guide has to be able to get along with people from all walks of life. A guide must be both a straight shooter and a straight talker.

Over the years, I developed an almost encyclopedic knowledge about everything around me. I knew the botanical names of the flora and fauna, from the most obvious tree to the most obscure little beetle. I learned all about firearms and ballistics all the while developing a deep understanding of domestic and international law related to the industry. I became proficient in first aid. If, while on a safari, one of my clients was attacked by a hippo or lion, tusked by an elephant, gored by a buffalo, or bitten by a snake, I had to be able to treat the casualty.

A lot of time was spent poring over books, listening to tapes and taking courses. There were written tests and multi-day practical examinations where we spent time out in the wild with our examiners. All of this was great and I learned a lot, but for me, the best learning was experiential and took place during my apprenticeship. I learned to share my knowledge of nature and to communicate effectively with people whether they were corporate CEO's from America, aid workers from Zambia, Muslims from Iran, or Catholics from Belfast.

I'll always remember getting licensed and taking my first group of clients on a safari. There was a middle aged German couple and two very attractive twenty-something Dutch girls. After everyone had gone to bed on the first night, I lay there in my sleeping bag on that little island in the middle of the Zambezi River. I started laughing quietly to myself as I thought about how I was getting paid to do something that I loved with all of my heart and soul.

I had fallen in love with the Zambezi River where I got to spend my days and nights sharing her mystery and magic with people from all around the world. I got to live the life of my dreams. Anyone I've ever introduced to my Zambezi mistress, anyone who's heard the cry of a fish eagle, survived the rush of a hippo or laid shivering in their sleeping bag listening to a lion roaring into the night, returned to their "other world" forever changed. They took with them a treasure trove of memories and at the same time, left behind a part of the person they were before.

The last year had been an interesting one. This was definitely not a job for the faint-hearted. Anything could happen at any time. As Stewart, my step-dad, was prone to point out, "Always expect the next animal to do everything you've ever read it won't do."

This outlook gleaned through his experiences in his early days in Africa, where as a young, naïve, idealistic Englishman, he'd come to Africa to save souls and to educate minds. He'd found himself in the middle of Zambia, on the border of the Barotse Floodplain, getting eaten by mosquitoes, teaching at the Mission Station where he and his friend, the local priest, would drink warm beer, save souls, educate minds and hunt buffalo to feed their flock.

His sage fatherly advice rang true on a number of occasions of late. Since the rains had broken, it seemed to me that the elephants, hippos, crocodiles and lions had formed a pact to terrorize me and had taken turns fulfilling their commitments. Even the honey badger, that tenacious little critter, appeared to be taking a little too much pleasure raiding my food supplies. I was always a little leery of these pests as they'd been known to kill buffalo, all two-foot nothing and thirty pounds of them. That they killed buffalo though, was not what grabbed my attention, but rather how they killed buffalo. They ripped out the genitals and the buffalo bled to death. But it wasn't the animals or the clients that drove me crazy. The bane of my life was poachers.

The no good liberals would argue that it wasn't the actual poachers who were evil. In fact, poachers were victims of the manipulative capitalists who dragged them from their villages, away from their day jobs as altar boys, and forced them to cross the border to kill our rhinoceros and elephants. Once they immobilized their prey, they hacked away at their still breathing, bleeding, agonized and terrified bodies to get the tusks or horns which would then be rushed across the world to be used by foreigners to make pretty little objects to please their geisha girls or as myth has it, to stimulate their erections.

I fully endorsed the "shoot to kill" policy our government had adopted to deal with these scum. In addition to killing our game, the poachers would also, given the opportunity, rob our safaris. After being robbed on two of the last three safaris I'd led, I'd had enough.

So it was time. We'd finished dinner; pasta served with a heavily garlic laden meat stew, gem squash on the side, and washed down with some white "nyala" wine, a cup of coffee and a wee dram of Port. The clients were pretty great and seemed to be enjoying their adventure. I was a little surprised that a foreigner, or FT (foreign tourist) as we called them, would choose to spend Christmas in a canoe, in the rain on the Zambezi. But hey, if they had the dream, I was more than happy to help them realize it.

Having discussed the probability that we'd be visited that night by the evil heathen hell poachers, as this was where they'd hit me on the two previous occasions, everyone mucked in to secure camp. Of particular amusement to everyone were the early warning booby traps we set around the canoes; pots, pans and anything else that we balanced, stuck, or wished into position would alert us to unsuspecting trespassers. Then, we dug a trench in front of my tent. This gave me a perfect field of fire as the poachers, aware of our country's policy towards them, now carried AK-47 assault rifles and had shown themselves more than willing to use them. I was taking no chances, and had no desire to get shot in the rain during Christmas.

"Ho bloody ho!" I chortled to myself as I reloaded my trusty Ruger Redhawk .44 magnum with soft nose rounds, removing the solids that would be more effective against a croc or hippo. Each guide had his own preference and mixed and matched rounds according to location, environment and personal preference. Solids or FMJ's (full metal jackets) would stay together when they went into something. Breaking up just a little bit, the brass coated lead bullet was very popular. The monolithic bullet was solid milled copper or brass, which really held together and was supposed to promote penetration. But, on that night, I wanted a soft nosed round. When that hit flesh, it splattered and ripped a big hole through whatever happened to be in its way. I wanted to make a mess of anyone who was shooting at me.

Taking turns to keep watch, Sean, my apprentice, and I were confident that we'd catch the fuckers. The rain had come and conditions were perfect for a confrontation. The clients' tents were strategically placed so as to minimize their exposure to gunfire. Because the heavily laden rain clouds snuffed out the stars, the only illumination came from occasional bolts of lightning that streaked across the sky. Something was not right. I looked across at the watchman, Sean. His soft snore alerted me that all was not well. There was definitely someone outside, and they were close by.

"God don't let me get shot!" I thought as I crept with my revolver in hand. I steeled myself for what might come. I launched myself out of the gaping opening of the tent, kicking Sean in the head as I ran into the pitch black rain. My dry, adrenaline-induced, metallic tasting mouth was not prepared for the agony about to burst through my body as my bare foot impaled itself on a poorly placed tent peg.

"Fuck, fuck, fuck, fuck!" Tears of rage mixed with the pelting rain ran down my face. The bolt of lightning revealed the tent peg embedded in my foot and the poachers getting away.

Not only had the fuckers stolen most of our food, but most of my booby-trap kitchen utensils too. Ho bloody ho, Merry Christmas and peace on earth to all mankind!

The best thing about safaris was that you always had the choice as to what kind of experience you were going to have. We couldn't control the weather and we couldn't control the animals but figured that we had a say in just about everything else. A little later that night as we hunched together under the tarpaulin, my foot a mess, most of the food gone, the rain pissing down, it would have been really easy to get upset and stop enjoying our grand adventure. We couldn't change what had happened but we talked about how we had complete control over how we responded to it. So we decided to make the most of whatever time we had left together. We still had some food. If we were willing to experiment, we could eat well. We were in the middle of paradise, albeit in the pouring rain, and we could create memories that would last a lifetime.

I'd love to say that the weather cleared up and we ate like kings, but it didn't end like that. It continued to piss down rain, my foot got infected, and the food was by and large barely edible. Against all that, we made sure that we shared a wonderful experience and created a trunk full of wonderful memories.

From time to time I've been able to live in the moment like that. The Sanskrit proverb penned by Kalidasa, an Indian poet and playwright, really resonated with me that day. If I stay in the day and the experience, everything seems to work out just wonderfully. It seems to me that when I try to get too involved in deciding what the projected outcome should be and why life is unfolding in a certain way, things seem to go to hell. The Zambezi, the poachers and the elements had conspired with Kalidasa to remind me that:

"Yesterday returneth not,
Perhaps tomorrow cometh not
The time is today, misuse it not...

Look to this day,
For it is life,
The very life of life.
In its brief course lie all
The realities and verities of existence,
The bliss of growth,
The splendor of action,
The glory of power...

For yesterday is but a dream,
And tomorrow is only a vision,
But today, well lived,
Makes every yesterday a dream of happiness
And every tomorrow a vision of hope.

Look well, therefore, to this day."

On many days, it is easier said than done.

I spent the next few years leading canoeing and kayaking safaris and white water rafting trips on the Zambezi River. I was also a part of the African experience with my clients whether on the back of a horse, in an open Land Rover and on foot, I loved it, but I also wanted more.

Mozambique, The First Time Around

Gary planted his foot just at the right spot between the bottom of my rib cage and my solar plexus, waking me up with a start. It was in conjunction with Dave screaming out expletives at the top of his voice, his Cumbrian accent turning "Those fucking heathen hells …" into "Theys faking haythan heyls …" alerting me that all was not well. My eyes slunk from Gary's beet red face to the waves crashing onto the beach. Our outdated map led me to believe that we were camped outside the little town of Macufi, Mozambique.

The three of us, Dave, Gary and I had worked together and apart on the mighty Zambezi River for a few years now with the same safari company. For reward or pleasure, we'd take whatever water craft the environment demanded – canoe, kayak or raft – and go exploring. Dave, an Englishman from Cumbria with the wiry build of a long distance runner, was one of the craziest guys I'd ever come across. Fearless wouldn't do him justice, because sometimes he would be scared shitless, but he'd still do the crazy-arsed things that only Dave could or would do in a kayak. In his element in huge white water, Dave had worked some of the most magnificent rivers around the world, feeding his addiction to adrenaline.

In Africa, wildlife photography had blossomed as a passion and Dave was quick on the way to becoming an accomplished photographer. It wasn't his proclivity to paddling insane lines that had earned him his nickname of "Flatliner Dave". No, that was due to the fact that one night Dave seemingly flat-lined after drinking too much Cane, a local spirit. A derivative of sugar cane, it was a little bit like vodka. As it turned out that night, Cane didn't like Dave as much as he liked it and he collapsed and stopped breathing. Once we knew why Dave had collapsed and stopped breathing, it was okay since we were all relatively competent in the art of bringing someone back from the other side with CPR. At first though, it freaked us all out.

Anyway, Dave and I drank way too much Cane the night before, and that he was still alive was, I felt, a cause for much celebration. Gary's mood on the other hand was one of consternation given that we were supposed to have kept an eye on things as he slept, but having passed out, we'd been negligent in our watchmen duties and had been robbed blind. Ordinarily, it wasn't that big of a deal, but the year was 1993 and we were in the middle of nowhere Mozambique, a country that was hopefully nearing the end of an incredibly brutal civil war.

Mozambique was raw; smarting from years of Portuguese colonization. There was little or no tourism industry. It was said that in the north, though heavily land-mined, it was teeming with wildlife - elephants, buffalo, zebras, giraffes … and unbelievable birdlife.

In addition to this, north of a place called Cabo Delegado was a chain of untouched islands. Not far off the coast separated from the mainland by blue waters atop pristine coral reefs, its only point of reference was that it rivaled the Great Barrier Reef. Apparently, cognizant of the role that tourism was to play in Mozambique's peaceful future, the government was willing to grant ninety-nine year leases to entrepreneurs willing to invest in developing their tourism industry. It was first come, first served.

It was said that the South Africans and anyone else with the cash to make it happen were lining up at the borders, awaiting the outcome of the current peace initiative. This was where I came in. As long as we could avoid getting shot, blown up or kidnapped and we could find some land and the appropriate authority to make a deal, we could get in ahead of the rest and pluck the prize right in front of their eyes. Dave had been easy to convince. He totally saw his future in Africa.

Gary hadn't taken much convincing either. His staff called him "Chimbure" after the tenacious honey badger. Five foot something tall, with a ruddy complexion, a full red beard and built like a brick, Gary's stocky build pronounced his immense strength. In love with the mighty Zambezi River in particular and the great outdoors in general, Gary was a great bushman. Hard as nails, he'd have to be killed to be stopped. It made him a must-have on a trip like this. But on this bright and sunny morning, as he chain-smoked, he was pissed at the pair of us.

Our plan was quite simple; stay out of trouble, be as inconspicuous as possible, don't stop unless you have to, hide as best you can at night, backtrack where appropriate and always have someone on watch. At first, I'd been all into it. I'd sit at night, armed with a crossbow enjoying the symphony of Africa, broken only by that very sudden silence; that total silence shrouded in darkness that comes just before dawn.

On February 14th, Gary, exhausted, had begged off the usual nightcap and had left Dave and I to it. There we were at this dot on the map, unique in that we'd finally made it to the coast and that for the first time in days, we actually knew where we were. The outdated map we had was midway between little and no use to us whatsoever. What looked like roads on the map according to the key/legend, was often a track at best. The well-traveled roads were pitted with ambush trenches, blow holes, and the macabre remains of previous travelers who'd either hit landmines or been ambushed, some disconcertingly recent. The towns and villages in general fared little better. Pock-marked walls bore testament to the battles that recently raged. Dead eyes scarred by scenes no person should ever gaze upon chilled us to the bone.

So there Dave and I were, spending Valentine's Day in Macufi. We raised our Cane-laden glasses in a toast to our current loved ones. It was apparent to both of us that our girlfriends deserved medals for putting up with us. It took us almost two sixty ounce bottles of Cane to stop trying to figure out why they bothered. After solving the world's problems, making sense of the universe and declaring undying love to our girlfriends, we then passed out. It was then that some industrious little punks had come and robbed us blind, stealing almost all of our food and much of our equipment. This was the scene that had greeted Gary that morning when he arose and accounted for my shortness of breath, pain below my ribs, throbbing head, and Dave's angst.

Fortunately, Gary had some emergency supplies, so we huddled around the campfire, slurping down a tin mug of hot, sweet, milky

Tanganda tea and made a plan to go to the nearby village and buy some more supplies. After a full days haggling, we departed dejected and really pissed off that we'd be driving off into the sunset with a lot less money than we had at sunrise. What made things worse was that we really didn't have much to show for the money we had spent. We embodied Dave's mantra "Make it harder!" In fact, it was biting us on the arse.

That night, huddled around our very little campfire beneath the canopy of billions of stars, aware that we were in the middle of a war zone, without enough food to last, we decided that we needed to be bolder. "Fuck 'em, it's war."

That night, I slept the deep sleep of the dead, awakening refreshed to African symphony Concerto No. 1. There was the sound of a pot being placed upon the coals on the fire, the melodious call of the cape turtle dove, beetles, bugs and all things African. God, I love that place.

"We need to stop for gas, boetman." I stated the obvious. The gas tank indicator had been hovering around empty for a while before just dying. It was getting a little tense in the cramped front of our little land cruiser.

"It's not good man, it's just not good." Gary spoke our thoughts. Our mood had flip-flopped from naïve enthusiasm to controlled terror as we seemed to have entered an area heavily populated by the resistance.

As we sped by, we'd see their surly forms, stalking through the bush, carefully avoiding the mined paths and roads, weighed down by their heavy loads of Kalashnikov assault rifles and RPGs, the simplistically sinister rocket launchers preferred by the combatants in guerilla warfare. The young and old were dressed alike in their ragged and mismatched uniforms of "freedom fighters" around the world. They were in their denim jeans, mandatory splashes of camouflage, khaki or olive drab, bandoliers or webbing, and the cold aura of death that shrouded them as closely as their sweat-stained garments.

To stop and be approached would not have a happy ending for our little bunch of unarmed, mobile, relatively well-supplied white guys. So, a few times a week when it was time to fill up with gas, we had to do a "hot refuel". First, we identified a rise in elevation where we could look out and around. If there were no "hostiles" spotted, we'd stop the truck with the engine idling, then leap out onto the back of the truck without setting foot on the mine-infested roadside while one of us opened the gas tank and sucked on the length of garden-variety hose-pipe; the other end of which had been placed into one of the 44 gallon drums of fuel that weighed down our truck. The seconds ticked away as the fuel gauge rose. Gary warned us when we were almost full, whereupon we'd cease refueling activities, close the fuel cap, and get the hell out of there as quickly as possible, as no good could possibly come from being a sitting duck.

As we sped off down the hill, relief gave way to a fit of giggles. I glanced into the rear-view mirror, instantly nauseated and turning a lighter shade of pale. The others didn't need to feel the anger that emanated from deep inside me to tell that something was wrong. Ahead of us, as far as the eye could see, lay a long, gently undulating hill. Straight as an arrow, the dirt road ran until its brown hues melded into a haze with the rest of the vegetation. Behind us, perched in the middle of the road, in the exact same spot in which we'd just refueled, clad in denim pants, and a cut off combat jacket, stood a "hostile". His denim cap askew made it easier for him to aim as he tracked our progress in the sights atop the tube of his rocket launcher.

I can vouch for a couple of clichés off the back of that experience. The hairs on the back of my neck rose and the sweat seemed to freeze as it ran down my spine. I also learned the meaning of the word helpless. We did the only sensible thing we could do. We kept on driving. He just stood there, tracking us with his rocket launcher, screwing with us. We briefly toyed with turning off the road; we wouldn't get too far in the truck, but we could at least make a run for it. Fortunately we didn't panic. Instead we kept on going, and thankfully, the "hostile" never let a rocket go. It never slammed into the back of our truck, exploding, igniting the fuel drums and either ripping us apart by force or burning us to a crisp.

We drove that "longest road" wasting the opportunity to do anything of perceived value, to make peace with our maker, or to ponder on the meaning of life. Instead, we spent those longest moments in camaraderie, cursing the elements that had conspired to bring us to this point, while at the same time, reveling in the opportunity to have lived such a life, wondering aloud if in fact it was time for us to be "Triple F'd' – Fucked by the Fickle hand of Fate". Faced with what we assumed was certain death, we celebrated life.

That night, as we all sat around the glowing embers of what had been a very little campfire, no one was talking much. We were all preoccupied with one thing or another. Sipping on a cup of tea, I went through a mini crisis. What was I thinking, not only being out here in the middle of hell, but having gotten these other two to join me on this harebrained adventure? What of their families and their futures? What of my family? Did the fact that I thought I was bullet proof give me the right to subject so many other people to the sadness that could inevitably follow? What was I thinking? As hard as I tried to beat myself up, I could only go so far, but I did feel for our families'concerns.

In a wine laced conversation with Mum some months prior to embarking on this adventure, she shared with me that, though she worried constantly at the lifestyle choices that I'd made, (which meant entering the Safari industry with its inherent risks, and the additional ones I created) she knew that I was happy and that I needed to satiate my thirst for adventure and for living on the edge. At the same time, I knew that she really hoped I would soon settle down, and as my family jokingly referred to it, "get a proper job". I listened, but knew I still had to drink more of life.

The following afternoon, having passed Cabo Delegado, we were in the zone. This was the area in which we were going to find our own little piece of paradise, and on it, start building our futures, making our fortunes, and living our lives. We were avoiding the landmine ridden roads, tracks, and paths as far as we possibly could. We instead chose to drive on the beaches, making detours when necessary.

Much of our recent hardship was quickly forgotten as we reveled in the splendor of the scenery and the beauty of the coastline. Here we were, the fine golden white seashell encrusted sands littered with palm trees meeting the ocean, crystal clear turning to dark blue. In some areas, it was calm. In others, the shore was battered by the incessant waves. The coral laden ocean floor, inhabited by cool, vivid, colorful fish stood between us landlubbers and the promise held on those little palm tree lined islands laying just off the coast.

We weren't seeing wildlife yet, but the bird life was spectacular. It was surpassed only by the marine life that we got to explore at night when we made camp. Having never dived near coral reefs before, I'd nothing to compare it to, and instead, I reveled in being blown away by the splendor of it all. Gary had spent some time diving in Australia and reckoned that it compared favorably with what he'd seen there.

Just when we got to thinking "This is the life", the heavens opened, and wave after wave of thunder rolled over us. Our world was illuminated by bolts of fire linking the heavens with the depths of hell and it rained. It wasn't a normal rain. It was torrential. For days! At first it was pretty cool as we got to replenish our water supplies, which had been running dangerously low, but after a while, it got real old. And then, it got downright nasty.

We came to a rocky point along the beach that we couldn't traverse in the truck, so we had to make a detour. We were not happy to leave the relative safety of the beach as we'd been warned to avoid the roads and paths in this particular area. Apparently, they were heavily mined. In no time, our vehicle had sunk up to its rear axle in nasty, muddy, black cotton clay soil. It was a mission from hell to extricate ourselves, but we did only to find ourselves in a similar predicament just a little while later. This time, it was worse. This time, we were well and truly stuck, going nowhere anytime soon.

When confronted by life getting in the way of our best laid plans, we did what most self-respecting explorers would do; we made some tea and assessed our situation. Gary's watch told the date, so we knew that we still had quite a few days left before we needed to be out of Mozambique. "Whatever you do," we'd been warned time and time again "do not overstay your visa unless you want to spend a very long time in a very shitty jail."

So time wasn't yet a concern. Our real concerns were that our vehicle was sunk above the axels in mud and we hadn't seen anyone for quite a while. The roads, tracks and paths were mined, and we were sitting in a declared "hostile" zone. Not to mention, it wouldn't stop fucking raining! We worked on trying to get the vehicle out for what felt like ages, to no avail. The one thing that I've found that you can pretty much guarantee in Africa is that if you sit somewhere long enough, someone will find you. So it happened that a group of fishermen found us some hours later, covered in sweat, mud and tears of frustration.

We released the truck from mother earth's firm embrace. Incredibly grateful, we gave our helpers some of our few remaining supplies and bid them a fond adieu as they spookily melted into the bush.

A few yards later, we almost sunk again. I went to get a machete out of the back of the truck only to find that our erstwhile saviors had in fact lightened our load considerably. I was pissed! I was pissed about the rain, the mud, the truck, about being robbed and pissed about everything else. I was also beginning to get more than a little nervous about the prospect of ever getting out of there.

We were all pissed, and it led to a dumb decision. There was an overgrown track running, no one knew where, but it looked as if it were going in the same direction we were. Dave and I, stripped down to our shorts, were to run on the tracks, guiding Gary in the truck. He was to stay back far enough so that he could react to any pitfalls that we pointed out along the way, as well as muddy bogs, holes, or God forbid, landmines we might trigger.

Off we went along the muddy earth. Each step of the way mud sucked our bare feet. The steady rain mingled with our sweat and cleansed our bodies as the adrenaline coursed through our veins giving us a heightened level of awareness. We ran like wild dogs that day, keeping up a steady pace, mile after mile. Every blade of grass and nook and cranny on the road was magnified, and we saw them with a clarity only experienced in dreams. As we ran, we joked about the absurdity of our situation, never knowing if the next step would result in a "kaboom!"

We wondered if we'd hear the click.

As the palm trees along the coastline bent to the winds from the sea, so too, we bent to what life had thrown at us. We were scared shitless, but at that point, faced with the alternatives, we knew that we really didn't have any other choice. By confronting those fears, we were more alive than we'd ever been before.

None too soon, we spotted a village perched atop a bluff with a magnificent view of the ocean. We followed our track into the village, rationalizing that if it was hostile, they knew about us by now, so what the hell? We pulled up into the center of the village. Once we fueled, Gary turned off the truck's engine, which seemed to be a cue for the rain to cease falling, the winds to quiet and for silence to envelop us.

We took tea time, and with a brew on the go, we took stock of our surroundings. It was a funny mix, this village. There were quite a few of the more commonplace round pole and dagga huts, but they weren't located in the usual haphazard manner. There appeared to be a method to the layout. The huts were laid out alongside regimented dormitories constructed with mud-baked bricks, palm frond roofs, and painted a kind of limestone white. In the center was something none of us had seen for quite a while, a well maintained gazebo in the middle of the village square. Something was afoot, but we couldn't find anyone.

With a cup of tea inside us and the temporary cessation of hostilities from the heavens above, the world was looking a lot better and, coupled with not being blown up or shot yet that day, relieved our spirits. Dave did one of the things that Dave does best. He started to sing. Dave is not only blessed with an amazing voice, but also with a capacity to remember (or, if necessary make up) the lyrics to more songs than your average pub jukebox.

He started with the well-known ballad "Danny Boy", his beautiful voice carrying through the village, and in that moment he became our pied piper. A little boy barely old enough to walk, dressed in a loincloth, clutching a piece of driftwood, came stumbling into view. He stood there, staring with wide-eyed fascination. Then, another little boy came by, then another, then a little girl, and then another.

Before long, Dave had an audience of ten, then twenty, and then even more. By now, the moms and dads were there too, some looking on gleefully, others with trepidation. Then, the guy who was obviously in charge, perhaps the chief, arrived and gestured Dave to continue. Dave ended his rendition of "Waltzing Matilda", then paused before resuming with "Mamma … just killed a man" which launched one of the songs we all knew, "Bohemian Rhapsody" by Queen. It had become something of a team song along the way, and we must have sung it hundreds of times. We joined him in a belting rendition of the classic, which won the crowd over as they rocked along with us.

When done, some pretty rangy looking warrior types approached us, and following time-honored traditions, they presented us to the chief.

Fortunately for us, it turned out that these were indeed "friendlies". The chief was a wizened old man with dancing eyes who didn't appear to be a day under four hundred and sixty-four years old. He had spent some time as a young man working in the diamond mines in Kimberley, South Africa. There, he had picked up, and could still remember, smatterings of the universal mine language Fanigalaw, a crude means of communication derived from Zulu, English, Afrikaans, Xhosa, and many other languages used to communicate and get work done.

As it had in yesteryear, on this grey and blustery day, Fanigalaw enabled us to communicate; we were welcome visitors to the chief, known from then on as "Chiefy." He assured us that we were the first white people that the vast majority of the villagers had ever clapped eyes on. We thought it was pretty cool, and so it was, as ambassadors of the rest of the world, we got to spend a few fun days listening to the chief and exploring his recommendations for the spot we were looking for.

Sitting there on the beach, I roared in celebration as the warm champagne splashed all over me. Before we started our trip, Mum had given us champagne and a tinned ham to celebrate with when we "found the spot". Mum was a great sport. With the benefit of hindsight, I can only begin to appreciate the days she must have spent in hell, wracked with the worry that I'd sentenced her to endure over the years as I'd gone about my life. So there Dave, Gary, Mum (represented by her goodies) and I sat and celebrated, dreaming of the future.

Now that we had found the spot and with the clock ticking and our visas nearing their expiration date, we decided that it was time to head home. We reasoned that if we started now, we could do it at a leisurely pace. As with all our other well-intentioned plans, it didn't take long for this one to start falling apart. After driving all day and pushing through the night, we crested a rise, and there, expecting to see a bridge over the Zambezi River, we were devastated to find that there wasn't one. It'd been blown up.

Joined by what I'm convinced were some of the largest, noisiest, most irritating mosquitoes on the face of the planet, was an equally annoying local who appeared out of seemingly nowhere, and gleefully assured us that we were in big trouble. There was no bridge, and due to the war effort, there was no way that we were going to get ourselves and our vehicle to the other side of the river and home.

What had a few hours earlier seemed like the last leg of our journey transformed into a cataclysmic mess. Stoking a fire to life so that we could get a cup of tea on the go, we assessed our situation. We had about forty gallons of fuel left, very little food, no hard currency, and very little time. Even if we had enough food and fuel, looking at the map, there was no way that we were going to make it to the border post separating Mozambique with Malawi before our visas ran out. Things were not looking good.

As the firelight illuminated the map that we were all staring at, willing a miracle, we saw a town that the key implied was the port city of Quellimane. Ports have ships. If we could get on a ship that would take us home, we might not end up in a dirty little third world jail cell for overstaying our visas. We had the better part of a week to come up with and execute a plan.

First off, we needed to establish that the town was still there, and that it wasn't some pock-marked scab on the face of Mozambique's haggard, war torn face. It wouldn't be the first time that we'd sought out a town from the map only to arrive at a terrible scene from an old war movie full of ravaged buildings and heavily populated with amputees. Amputees who served as a constant reminder to us not to take a step more than we absolutely had to on Mozambiquan soil as it was littered with landmines. That was going to be an obstacle to attracting tourists. We needed to clear all the mines around the camp. After all, a tourist standing on a mine and getting blown up would surely mess up any marketing strategy we might come up with.

As we drove through downtown Quellimane, our spirits soared. Armed with directions to Navique's office, I could almost taste Mum's celebratory home-cooked dinner of rare roast beef, roast potatoes with Yorkshire pudding, cauliflower cheese, peas and lashings of gravy with horseradish and mustard on the side.

Navique, it turned out, was Mozambique's national shipping line. The officious little bastard at the office, the only one fluent in English assured us, "Yes, we could put our vehicle and ourselves on a ship. In fact, the good ship Mwanza was due to sail the next day. Yes, we'd get to Beira with time to spare giving us plenty of time to enjoy the direct six hour drive to the Zimbabwe border and home. Yes, we had enough money in Zimbabwe dollars to pay for it all. But no, they wouldn't take Zimbabwean dollars."

No amount of begging and pleading would get the unhelpful little prick to relent and take our dollars. In fact, the more we pleaded, the higher the price went.

Making our way to the bank, we started giggling; we were all starting to come a little unglued. Waltzing into the bank, we decided that Dave, with his good old English accent, was to do the talking. Standing in line behind us was one of only a small handful of English speaking people within hundreds of miles. We told him about our predicament and he just clucked his tongue in sympathy and said "Shame."

Standing outside the bank, we were approached by the English speaking chap from inside. "Go see Mr. Mohamed," he urged us. "He sick. He go to Zimbabwe. Maybe he can help."

With nothing to lose, we got directions to where we might find Mr. Mohammed, and we set off. Driving along the palm-lined promenade, you couldn't help but imagine this town as it once was.

Many miles later, the sun not far from setting over the ocean, we finally tracked down the elusive Mr. Mohamed, and yes, he was sick. He didn't speak English but his assistant spoke smatterings of French. What transpired was nothing short of amazing to me. In broken conversation laced with acted out scenes, not unlike charades, we established that yes he was sick, very sick and that he was planning on going to Harare in Zimbabwe to seek medical treatment.

We managed to convey our dire situation and he offered me the money in hard currency to secure our passage, urging me to hang onto the cash we had as we might yet need it. He asked only for a phone number to call when he got to Harare whereupon he would be reimbursed nothing more and nothing less than he was lending us. We never did find out what exactly was wrong with our benevolent savior, "Tummyache", as we affectionately referred to him thereafter. We gratefully took the unsecured loan, and set off back to town, camping that night on the bank of one of the many rivers that seemed to feed into the ocean.

Dave and I, too highly strung to sleep, decided to tempt fate one more time. We would swim across the river, cut through the sleeping village undetected, and make our way to the ocean. We did it for the adventure, and because we thought that we were bulletproof. I said a quick prayer to the gods asking that we not be eaten by any crocs or any other manner of potential ugliness that might be about, and we launched ourselves into the river. Immediately we were lit up like a firework display, fluorescent greenish yellow, as we stroked our way across the water, our every movement reacting with the plankton to produce the effect.

Not only were we visible to any man-eating creature that might be up and about, but our stealthy, let's-get-in-and-out-of-the-village plan had gone to the dogs, who started barking and barking. We were in a time and place where dogs barking at strange people in the middle of the night didn't amount to much good, often unleashing a fusillade of small arms fire. Our adrenaline-charged bodies lay still until the dogs quieted down and the village rested once more. We swiftly and carefully made our way to the ocean, and high on life, we played in the water for hours. Our screams were drowned out by the crashing moonlit waves as we celebrated life and watched the sun rise from the water and light up the palm-lined beach.

Reluctantly, we headed back to camp. As I dove back in to cross the river, I quickly realized that something was wrong. The tide had changed and what had been an easy swim in calm water a few hours earlier, was now a battle against a strong current. Midway across the river, it dawned on me that it was a battle that I might not win. The water was sapping my strength and I was starting to panic a bit, and considered the possibility that I may in fact be about to meet my maker.

Then, out of nowhere, appeared a couple of fishermen in a mkoro, a dugout canoe. They rescued me and dropped me off on the bank with Dave and Gary who, in between chastising me for my foolishness and calling me a jackass, were getting mileage with the fishermen. They reenacted the panicked expression on my face and my flailing arms during what I thought were my last moments on earth. Once everyone had settled down, we thanked the fishermen for rescuing me. I gave them my penknife and anything else that I thought they might find useful and we set off for Quelimane and our ride home.

With money, we went back to the office and saw the same little bastard from the day before. We agreed upon a fare, paid it, and made our way down to the wharf, where, with much relief, we drove our vehicle onto the good ship Mwanza. Before long, we would head south to Beira, and then home.

Castro, the five foot something, English speaking first officer spelt out what we could expect over the next day or so. We'd follow the coastline and be in Beira by noon the next day. We'd not see the Captain as he would be busy in his cabin shagging some woman, not his wife, to within an inch of her life. She appeared kind of skanky and was something of a screamer, but I didn't really care. I was atop the freighter throwing my guts up over the side of the ship. It was in the midst of this that I realized that I could no longer see land. That I was seasick was one concern. That this bucket of a boat could stay afloat on the high seas was quite another.

Upon questioning, Castro informed us that another of Navique's boats had broken down and we were going to find it and tow it back to Beira with us. "Don't worry," he assured us, "it's not too far out of the way."

Some hours later, I was in no doubt whatsoever that I was in the process of being "Triple F'd", Fucked by the Fickle hand of Fate, again. We found the other boat, but it was really a ship, not a boat. The crew went ahead with securing a line from our ship to their ship. It was a little too secure as it turned out. The dead calm sea gave way to something I'd previously only had nightmares about. I'd never been in a hurricane before. I laid on the floor of the pilot-house, wet and exhausted. I was one hundred and twenty plus feet above the waterline, and waves were crashing all around. Everything about the scene was wrong. We'd passed beyond hell.

The storm had hit us incredibly fast. The water whipped up into a series of gigantic swells with the ships subjected to a two-pronged assault from wind and sea. The deadweight we were towing and were unable to release was providing some entertainment. Were it not so absolutely out of control, it might have been amusing. We'd crest a wave, the line taught, and as we dove, the other ship would come diving right behind us. Then, everything would disappear under water, and it would happen all over again.

At some point, the umbilical cord broke, and we, the mother ship, were all alone. Though I couldn't speak Portuguese, it was obvious that we were in the shit as the terrorized crew, summoning everyone below deck, battened down the hatches. I'd had enough. Convinced that the end was nigh, I decided I wasn't going to be caught like a rat below deck when this bucket went down. I grabbed my sleeping bag and fought my way back up to the pilot-house. I pulled my sleeping bag over my head, screamed

"See you in Heaven", and promptly went to sleep. My last prayer was that it would be quick, not too scary and not too painful.

So when Dave woke me the next morning with a cuppa tea, I was well chuffed. We were amazed that we'd eluded the Grim Reaper yet again. Given all that I lived through that night, I'm convinced it was the closest that I've ever come to death.

The ship we'd been towing was nowhere to be seen and Castro really didn't want to talk about it. The rest of the crew was walking around with the bemused expression of survivors who can't quite believe they're still alive. The giggly mood was infectious. We had all survived. Dave, Gary and I were invited to the galley to join the rank and file in their frugal meal. Somehow, the previous nights experience had forged a bond between us all. It was a camaraderie enjoyed only by those who have been to the very edge together and then, having looked death squarely in the eye, made it back. I wish I could say that our relationship improved with the officers, but they became even more hostile.

As we headed towards the shore, we should have known better than to believe our adventure was almost over. The Port of Beira is nested on the Pungwe river estuary. The second largest port in Mozambique, it boasts twelve quays. Beira has always been a transit port, handling the import and export cargoes from Zimbabwe, Malawi, Zambia and other countries in the region. The port's entrance is about twenty nautical miles from the open water along the dredged sixty-meter wide Macuti channel, which has buoys and lighting to guide ships in.

The first sign that things were not as they should be was when we dropped anchor, and the Captain and his floozy, making a rare appearance, climbed off the good ship Mwanza and onto the boat that had arrived to take them ashore. Castro at first pretended that this was normal, that we'd be onto shore before long and back in Zimbabwe with days to spare. Day turned into night. Night turned into day. By now, we were being told that if we were to pay a certain amount, then we could come in. If not, we'd just have to stay where we were with our visas about to expire. Frustration, boredom, fear, loathing, confusion, irritation, outrage, exasperation, the blend of moods, thoughts and emotions pissed us off and we were done.

We "jumped ship" onto a tender boat and made it to the port. Quayside, oozing desperation, we succeeded in soliciting a cab ride close to the Zimbabwe embassy. Once the cab dropped us off, we were three deranged mukiwas (white people) charging with wanton abandon through the streets of downtown Beira. We somehow managed to end up in front of Mr. Makombe, the Zimbabwean High Commissioner, who learning of our plight, went about resolving it. It was a wonderful moment when we stormed the head of Navique's office and Mr. Makombe informed the official that, on behalf of the Zimbabwean Government, he was prepared to institute proceedings against the company for an array of charges including piracy and abduction.

The official got the message loud and clear and within a couple hours, the ship was docked and our vehicle was off-loaded.

With ten hours to spare, we crossed the border into Zimbabwe. Five hours later, we pulled up at my parent's house. That night, we celebrated. We drank lots of red wine, Dave drank lots of Cane and didn't flat line, and we ate rare roast beef, roast potatoes with Yorkshire pudding, cauliflower cheese, peas and lashings of gravy with horseradish and mustard on the side.

We never did open shop in Mozambique. The civil war ended, and peace and new governance came to the land. The warring parties came together in what at least on the surface, appeared to be a government of National Unity.

Dave, Gary, and I returned to our lives in Victoria Falls. I got to pursue my entrepreneurial bent by setting up a safari consulting operation which as it turned out, I absolutely loved. Within a year, I had transformed an idea into a successful safari operation named San Simba Safaris. I had a great team working with me and I was convinced that we were doing something pretty special.

Going Solo in the Safari Business

San Simba was not only my first successful safari consulting venture, but also the one of which I am most proud. We offered various safari experiences, the most popular being the Royal Drift, a luxury canoe trip down a magnificent stretch of the Zambezi River.

Looking back to the day we launched the Royal Drift, my paddlers were ready. Max, a close, lifelong friend of mine and fellow river guide, had come along for the ride to provide moral support to me and coaching support to some of my paddlers. All was going really well. I was in the lead boat and we were right near the end of the trip. I really couldn't have asked for anything more from Nyami-Nyami, the river god.

The sun was setting; the sky was blue with hues of orange, red and purple. Just ahead, the mist rose off Victoria Falls. The birdlife and wildlife had put on a real show. The flora and fauna had won the day, and it was with reluctance that I was to end this inaugural trip. In the lead boat, my elderly Spanish clients and I had shared a few broken conversations. Mostly though, they'd been more than content to sit back and revel in being a part of something quite marvelous, greedily soaking up the splendor that nature had to offer.

Then, suddenly breaking that perfectly peaceful moment, our canoe started to tilt, gently at first, and then more and more until, as if in slow motion, we toppled over. "Shit!", I thought, "not good."

I wasn't overly concerned yet. I was more confused. When I made it to the surface, I saw that Mrs. Spaniard was pretty freaked out, so I grabbed a hold of her and dragged her to the bank, calling to Mr. Spaniard.

All the while, Mr. Spaniard had become somewhat disoriented and was swimming in the wrong direction, towards the upturned canoe.

Then, out of nowhere, a hippo hit the upturned canoe and shifted his focus to Mr. Spaniard, chomping the water to froth and heading straight towards him. Mr. Spaniard definitely wasn't listening to me now; he was overwhelmed and incapacitated by terror at the approaching hippo. I dove in, grabbed a hold of him, and as the hippo tore the water up all around us, I dragged him to safety. The hippo did no harm except scare the hell out of us. He went about hitting the boat a few more times for good measure, and then disappeared. Thank God Max had been on that trip. His professionalism and testicular fortitude while helping me recover equipment and settle the clients went a long way towards saving the day.

Coming home at the end of this rather eventful day, as I strolled up my driveway, Solo, my pet black cat, rushed to meet me. It was our little routine. Solo would wait on the step for me to come back from safari if he wasn't busy chasing Scruffy, my housemate and dear friend, James', little dog around the yard. Solo was a bedraggled few days old orphan when we found him. Jess, my girlfriend, set about nursing the little thing back to life. She tried to feed him porridge through a syringe but he'd have none of that. We thought for sure that he'd die and discussed that eventually when I spotted him scaling the plate that had part of a leftover ham sandwich on it. He started chowing down. The cat lived, and we became firm friends.

Stooping over to pet Solo, I made my way up to the step where Jess and a handful of housemates and friends were gathered enjoying a sundowner.

"Heard you got chomped," James intoned, "Way to launch a new company!" He cracked, clearly having already heard via the "bush telegraph" what had occurred earlier that day on the river. Of course, the fact that I had obviously been wet from head to toe was also a bit of a clue that something had gone awry on a typically perfect day in Africa.

Everyone except Jess laughed at James' comment. James was of course referring to the fact that on the day that I launched San Simba Safaris, I had a run-in with a hippo.

As I told the tale, Dave, nursing a Cane and Coke, and James and Mike McNamara, known as Mac, sipping their beers, wondered aloud at what the hippo had been thinking. This was certainly very unhippo-like behavior. Given that they were all veterans on the mighty Zambezi, I was relieved to hear that they thought the way I thought.

There would be six other guides and their clients who'd have run-ins with the brute in the months that lay ahead. Mac and I obviously had no inclination that a few months down the line, we'd soon be involved in one last encounter with the hippo.

Chapter 4

The Attack

The Hippo Attack
March 1996

"Welcome to the mighty Zambezi," I began. "The trip you're taking today is called the Royal Drift because we do the paddling and your job is to sit back, relax and enjoy the magnificent scenery of Africa. The hardest part of your day will be leaning over to get a snack or turning around to ask for another gin and tonic."

The six tourists – or clients, as we in the tourism industry refer to them – sat on the black cotton clay of a small riverside clearing, facing the river. My three apprentice guides and I stood on the bank facing the clients; the only thing between them and the river. The safety talk, given on shore before launching the boats, is critical to a successful river trip. The trick is to imbue the clients with a sense of respect for the river and its dangers while not scaring the hell out of them.

Each river guide has his own style and brand of showmanship and I liked to ease into my safety talk with a brief geography lesson.

"At 1,600 miles, the Zambezi is the fourth-longest river in Africa, after the Nile, the Niger and the Congo. The river before you is born 700 miles north of here as a tiny ribbon of water bubbling up from the ground in a remote, unsettled corner of Zambia. It gradually broadens to a width of 400 yards and gathers power as it flows south through Angola and back into Zambia. Approximately 250 miles north of where we're standing, the river spills out across the Barotse flood plain, stretching to some 20 miles across at its widest point during the flood season."

There were three couples, all in their 30's – Murielle Fischer and her fiancé, Pierre Lagardere, their friends Nathalie Grassot and Marc Skorupka, who were employees of Air France enjoying a week-long layover in Africa and Jochem Stahmann, an automotive engineer and his wife, Gundi, from Bremen, Germany.

I scanned their faces. All had that look that was familiar to me from five years of guiding on the Zambezi; an edgy mix of anticipation and creeping fear, like the frightened fascination of a child who has finally reached the front of the line for the roller coaster. This was normal. My job was to reassure everyone that if they followed my directions, they would be completely safe.

"The stretch of river we're about to explore is one of the most magnificent settings in all of Africa. We will be treated to some of the greatest bird watching on earth. The wildlife population here is dense – expect to see elephants, hippos, crocodiles, impala and perhaps a lion or a Cape buffalo or two."

Everyone was paying keen attention at this point, particularly the German woman, anxiety etched in her face. I had to proceed carefully.

"The river and its inhabitants can be violent so you must be aware of the dangers, of which there are four main ones."

I paused for effect.

"The first danger," I intoned ominously, "is the sun." Relieved grins creased everyone's face, my cue to continue. "The African sun is vicious so keep your hats on your heads and sunblock on exposed body parts. Nothing will ruin your holiday quicker than a severe sunburn.

"The second danger is submerged stumps and rocks. If you feel a thud on the bottom of your canoe, but aren't thrown from your seat, we've run into a submerged obstacle. If the boat gets caught on the stump or rock, the current will spin the boat sideways so that you'll be facing one of the banks. If this happens, ignore the natural tendency to lean upstream and instead lean downstream. This will prevent the current from grabbing the side of the boat and flipping it over.

"The third danger is hippos." I grinned, careful not to seem cocky. The clients leaned forward. The growing sense of terror emanating from the German woman was now almost palpable – the kind of fear that can quickly turn contagious. I had to make sure the fear didn't overwhelm her – a gibbering wreck on a canoe safari is not only bound for an unpleasant African wilderness experience, but is a potentially mortal liability should something go wrong on the water.

"Hippos are territorial animals, so as well-trained veteran guides, we know which areas to avoid. But a hippo having a bad day might decide to bump your canoe. If you feel a thud on the bottom of the boat and are then launched from your seat, you've been hit by a hippo. If you land back in your seat and the boat is still upright, no worries, you're in good shape. Sit tight and rest assured that your guide will be paddling with great urgency away from the hippo. Hippos typically hit a boat just once and then swim immediately for deep water. They want as little to do with us as we do with them."

Keeping in mind that the goal of a safety talk is to make the clients aware of the river's hazards while not paralyzing them with fear, full disclosure regarding hippos is not advisable. A pissed-off hippo presents a life-or-death situation, and most everybody in Africa who has spent any time near a river can relate at least one true story of a hippo attacking some fisherman or canoeist, invariably with very poor results for the human. But steering clear of hippo territory is a relatively simple thing, and Zimbabwean river guides are trained to avoid such occurrences. The fact is that more often than not Zambezi River trips come off without a hitch, and the odds are slim of an unwanted encounter with a hippo or any other beast ending in casualties.

That doesn't mean that these encounters never happen. I shared the story of how six months earlier, I was guiding an elderly Spanish couple on this very trip and had a run in with a particularly gnarly hippo.

That incident turned out to be the first of several attacks by this particular hippo, an ornery rogue bull who, six months later, was still terrorizing boats around Vic Falls without provocation. But he had staked out his area of the river, and all the river guides knew where it was. Needless to say, I planned on giving that anti-social bastard a wide berth.

With everyone's rapt attention, I continued the safety talk.

"It is possible that a hippo may capsize your boat. Should that happen and you find yourself in the water, listen very closely to me. This will be easy, as I will be screaming at the top of my lungs. The main thing is not to panic; just listen to me. Don't worry about the hippo eating you; hippos are vegetarians. They don't like meat."

Armed with the false comfort that hippos are strictly plant-eaters, most clients relax a bit. But every once in a while, someone in the group, usually a male, will announce in a know-it-all tone of voice, "I've heard hippos kill more people in Africa than any other animal."

"Yes," I'd respond quickly, "I've heard that as well. I've also heard that those killed by hippos are most often poachers trying to capture and kill them, or fishermen knocked from their makoros who are not attacked but end up drowning because they can't swim."

There were no such know-it-alls in this crowd, however, and I wanted to proceed quickly with the rest of the talk as the German woman was looking quite anxious.

"If you are knocked into the water, I will bring either the front or rear of my canoe to you. Do not try to climb over the side and into the boat because you'll tip it over and then I'll be in the water with you and we'll all be in a real mess."

I paused once more for effect while I stared bluntly into each set of eyes, one at a time.

"If you do try to climb over the side of my canoe, I will beat you about the head and hands with my paddle until you let go."

I looked impassively at each of them, to reinforce the seriousness of this point.

"The fourth danger is crocodiles. The Zambezi is full of them. Crocs won't attack anything bigger than they are and these canoes are slightly longer than the biggest one in the area."

A few nervous chuckles.

"Don't trail your hand in the water. It will look like a fish and that's what crocs snack on. Now, you're probably thinking, "If a hippo knocks us into the water, we'll be fair game for a croc.

"Rest assured," I continued, "it's extremely unlikely that any self-respecting croc will get within a mile of an upset hippo. Hippos are known for chomping crocs in half. But should there be a croc nearby, you'll probably get eaten, and I won't be coming to help. Just look at it as … having a particularly bad day."

For some reason that I've never understood, that always loosened them up.

"Any questions?" I asked.

"Why do you carry a gun?" asked Murielle.

I lifted the holstered .357 Magnum at my side. "So that I can prevent a mutiny at the end when I tell you all that the trip is over." Laughter all around.

"OK folks, one last thing. I need you all to sign this indemnity form before we set off."

As the adventurers scribbled their signatures on the forms, Jochem, the frightened woman's husband, sidled up to me.

"My wife, Gundi, she's a bit nervous," he said. "Two years ago we were on a Zambezi canoe trip and our boat was chased by a hippo."

"No problem," I told him. "You two ride in my boat. You'll be safe with me."

While the three couples gathered their cameras, video camcorders and sunscreen, I huddled with my three apprentices. Ben Sibanda, 24, and Evans Namasango, 22, who had worked in the safari industry for years as camp hands and porters and were studying to become guides. Mac was a seasoned bushman and was accompanying us in his kayak to log river hours toward his formal river guide certification.

As Ben and Evans dragged the canoes toward the water's edge, and Mac carried his kayak, I ran through a final check of the equipment. The two-way radio and first aid kit were secured in the Pelican case, a bright orange briefcase made of crushproof, airtight, watertight, shockproof plastic. Then I checked my personal kit – the standard river guide outfit of khaki shorts, a hunter's green, long-sleeved shirt, a baseball hat of the same color, black-strapped Teva sandals and my lucky Ray Ban sunglasses. I had become so attached to this particular pair of "sunnies" over the years that last Christmas, Mum simply replaced the lenses for me rather than buy a new set of glasses, which might have upset the karma of good fortune I believed emanated from this pair.

Sheathed at my waist was my Kershaw hunting knife, the Rolls Royce of bush knives, with a six-inch blade and molded, black rubber handle.

The final step of my preparation ritual before getting on the water was to adjust the shoulder holster that holds my .357 Magnum. I tugged the straps, apparently too hard – the buckle of the harness broke, rendering it useless. Well, there was no time to fix it now as the clients were climbing into the boats. I slid the holster off the harness and attached it to the belt around my waist.

Our three canoe armada set off. Jochem and Gundi rode with me in the lead canoe; Murielle and Pierre went with Ben; Nathalie and Marc rode with Evans.

We bobbed along in the 18-foot, sky-blue Canadian style canoes as a cooling wind drifted over the river. Ben, Evans and I paddled from the back of our canoes, with one client near the bow, the other in the middle of the boat. Lounging in the plastic seats molded to the floor, the three couples propped their arms on the sides of the boat and stretched their legs. To accommodate the large coolers and snack trays stacked in the boats, Ben, Evans and I sat cross-legged.

The sun radiated from a cloudy, milky blue sky. We meandered around tiny islands and through the tree-lined channels of the river. Here, just upstream of the Falls, rock formations and grass-covered islands jut out from the Zambezi, turning the river into a maze of channels and small pools. We drifted lazily past towering reed beds, a profusion of papyrus and golden fragmites while egrets, cormorants, fish eagles, rollers and bee eaters flitted about overhead. Downstream, clouds of mist hung above the river, shot skyward where the Zambezi swan dives over Vic Falls and drops 355 feet – twice the height of Niagara Falls – into the gorge below.

After an hour or so on the water, and several cocktails, everyone had settled down to enjoy the scenery. Clutching their drinks and munching sausage rolls, chicken wings, cheese and salads, the Europeans hollered excitedly across the boats to one another while pointing their camcorders to and fro. At one point, a bull elephant stepped from the bush on an island less than 10 yards from us, fanning his ears forward and back as he eyed us before dropping his head slowly for a long slurp from the Zambezi.

Several pods of hippos waded shoulder-high in the river's shallows or sunned themselves on the small islands. There had been no disruptions all afternoon. Everyone was having a wonderful time, and any fears that had surfaced during the safety talk seemed to be forgotten. They were now replaced by the soul-soothing tranquility of the Zambezi and her lush, tawny and green banks teeming with wildlife.

I glanced at my watch. It was now just after 5:00 pm. Forty more minutes of drifting and laid-back paddling before we would meet the Land Rover that would return the clients to their hotel.

We paddled slowly along the shoreline of a tree-covered island and watched a pod of a dozen hippos. With only their heads above the water, they stopped their nuzzling and shuffling, stood statue-still and stared right back at us as we glided past.

While the clients and hippos watched each other, I caught the attention of the three apprentices and motioned to a small island 200 yards directly downstream. There, on the island's shoreline, was a mother hippo with her calf.

I directed the clients' attention downstream, pointing out mom hippo and baby. "A mother hippo with a calf is to be avoided at all costs," I said. "They are extremely protective of their young and will not hesitate to attack a canoe they think is too close."

I rapped my paddle on the edge of the canoe three times. "Submerged hippos in the area hear the pounding and usually surface to see what all the noise is about," I explained to Jochem and Gundi, "allowing us to steer clear. You want to give hippos as much warning as possible as to your whereabouts, as they dislike surprises. You want to always allow them access to the deep water, which is where they usually go to avoid boats.

"If you get between the river's deep water and a hippo lingering near shore, chances are good the animal will go through you to get to where he wants to go, a most unpleasant situation."

As the canoes and Mac's kayak spread out from each other, I chatted with the Germans about hippos. "Hippopotamus is a Greek word meaning river horse," I said. "The bulls can grow to be 15 feet long, five feet high and 8,000 pounds. Hippos are the second largest terrestrial mammals; only elephants are larger."

"That's more than my BMW," laughed Jochem. He sipped a gin and tonic while Gundi trained her binoculars on a hippo wading in the center of the river.

We angled river-left, away from the hippo and her calf. My plan was to continue toward the left bank for 50 yards or so, going around the island where the hippo and her calf were wading, then continue downstream through the channel to the left of the island. I yelled to Mac, now in the lead in his 6-foot kayak. "At the end of the channel, bear left and go around the pool up ahead." Mac gave a thumbs-up.

Mac, Ben, Evans and I were well aware that the rogue hippo's established territory was a quarter mile ahead. We would alter our course once we were another 100 yards downstream.

We had no way of knowing that the hippo had relocated, and that we were on a collision course with his new stomping ground.

I kept an eye trained on the mother hippo some 50 yards away as she stared at the canoes; her tiny, golf ball-sized ears twitching atop her massive head. The scenery here was spectacular. The clients had gone quiet in the dusky twilight, listening to the hypnotic water song of the Zambezi. The cruise was going beautifully as was almost always the case with the afternoon cruise. The clients' apprehensions had evaporated in the brilliant March sunshine like the mist rising from the plummeting waters of Victoria Falls.

We were now in the homestretch. We'd been on the water for two-and-a-half hours, and in about 30 minutes would head to shore, where a Land Rover would be waiting to shuttle the Europeans the three miles back to their hotel in town for "sundowners," the Zimbabwean cocktail hour. Ben and Evans would head home while Mac and I would head to Explorer's Bar, where the river guide fraternity gathered to cap a day's work with a night of drinking and story-swapping.

We were now far left of mom hippo and her cute baby, so I steered downstream, headed for the narrow channel that would take us past the two hippos at a safe distance. As I entered the mouth of the channel, I looked behind to make sure all the boats were in tight formation. Ben's canoe was right behind me, with Mac paddling alongside him, chatting with the clients. Evans had dropped back a bit, some 30 yards behind. To give him a chance to catch up, I set my paddle down. "Anyone for a last cocktail?" I asked Jochem and Gundi.

An ear-splitting crack exploded the evening stillness. Even as I swiveled my head around to look, I knew the sound. I turned to see Evans catapulted from the rear of his canoe four feet into the air. The boat was still upright with the two tourists seated inside, but it was suspended a foot above the water, resting on the leathery brown back of a massive bull hippo – the very bull hippo that had attacked me and the Spaniards six months ago and was supposed to be a quarter of a mile away from here.

Evans shot through the air in what seemed to be slow motion. His passengers, Nathalie and Marc, gripped the sides of the wobbling canoe, trying to steady it as Evans splashed into the water in front of them as if dropped from the sky. Evans disappeared beneath the water's surface. The hippo submerged, letting the rear of the canoe slap down onto the water and rocking Marc and Nathalie wildly from side to side. They managed to avoid capsizing. Then, Nathalie began screaming. Evans popped to the surface, his arms flailing and terror in his eyes. The languid serenity of a moment ago was gone, replaced by chaos, women screaming and the sick feeling one gets watching tragedy unfold.

"Hold on Evans, I'm coming," I yelled, frantically paddling backwards. Evans was a competent swimmer, but for some reason he beat the water uselessly while the current dragged him straight toward the mother hippo and her calf.

There was a large rock, as big as a living room, jutting above the water 20 yards away from us. "Ben, get everyone to that rock," I shouted as I sped past his canoe.

Paddling hard, I scanned the rapidly decreasing distance between Evans and the mother hippo. It would have been faster to turn the canoe around and paddle towards Evans' bow first, but I wanted to keep the clients as far from harm as possible. Should the striking hippo reappear, I wanted to be between him and them.

I strained against the paddle, angling my strokes to stay on course. Glancing to my left, I yelled instructions to Ben, but there was no need. He was 50 yards away, toward the left bank, dropping his clients off on the big rock that rose two feet above the water. Murielle and Pierre stepped quickly from their canoe. Ben spun the boat around and paddled toward Marc and Nathalie, who were hand-paddling in a frenzy toward the rock where Murielle and Pierre now stood. Ben pulled alongside and towed them the final 20 yards to the rock.

Evans was barely keeping his head above water. I noticed something in the water. A thin v-shaped bow wave crested the water's surface, moving toward me at rapid speed. That type of bow wave is unmistakable – it's the ripple of the water surface made by a submerged, fast-moving hippo. The son of a bitch was now coming for my canoe.

I slapped my paddle hard on the river's surface as the arrowhead of water bore down on us. This is standard procedure for scaring off hippos, and an extremely effective procedure at that. Though it seems like a pathetic attempt to ward off a charging, four-ton beast, I'd never seen the practice not work. Still beating the water, I hoped this particular creature had read the book on hippo behavior. The bow wave kept coming, closing in like a torpedo.

Then it disappeared. The hippo changed his mind, thank God, and dove to deep water. Okay for now, but the only thing worse than an angry hippo that you can see is one you can't see.

I was now ten yards from Evans, who was gasping and on the verge of shock. "Sit tight, Evans, we'll have you out in just a few seconds," I yelled.

I maneuvered the canoe next to Evans, who in his panic forgot the part of the safety talk wherein it is strongly advised not to attempt entering the side of the canoe. As he reached to grab the right side of the boat, I yelled, "No, grab the back!" and executed a swift stroke to pull the rear of the canoe within his reach. I dropped my paddle into the boat, twisting my upper body to the right to reach over the back of the boat and grab Evans' outstretched hand. "Lean to the left!" I snapped to Jochem and Gundi. I needed them to counterbalance my weight as I stretched my right arm over the stern.

My arm was fully extended; the canoe drifted gently into place so Evans could grasp my hand. He readied himself. My body hung out over the water from the waist up as I strained to reach just a bit further. His arm was thrust out of the water as the current pushed the canoe the last few inches toward him. I looked along the length of my arm, my outstretched hand inches from Evans. Just another two inches …

As our fingers almost touched, the water between us erupted.

The world went dark and quiet. "Where am I?" was the second thought to go through my mind, "Oh shit!" having been the first. A massive blur had boiled up out of the water between me and Evans, but what was it? Entombed in darkness and surrounded by an awful, putrid smell that can only be described as death, I tried to figure out what in the hell was going on.

My legs felt differently than the rest of me. From the waist up I was … not dry … but not surrounded by water as were my legs. And an unbelievable pressure was bearing down on my lower back, like I was being squeezed in a vice.

The situation crystallized in my mind. The hippo had swallowed me headfirst up to my waist. That's why my legs felt differently than the rest of me – from the waist up, I was face down in the gullet of a hippo! Adrenaline and panic flooded my brain.

I wriggled and shook, struggling to break free, but aside from my legs, I couldn't move. My arms were pinned, the right one alongside my body, the left one at a right angle to my torso. The pressure on my back intensified. I felt two pops in my lower back, like a hot dog being stuck by a fork.

I thrashed my legs, trying to escape the dank, slimy hold. The bull released its grip. I was free, carried along underwater by the current. Though oblivious to pain or injury, I was on the verge of suffocating. I stroked for the water's surface, fighting off the panic and fear of drowning. My head popped out of the water and I gasped, sucking air. The first thing I saw was Evans, still treading water desperately and not all together successfully. "Let's get out of here," I rasped.

But Evans continued to thrash in the water. His eyes were now vacant and far away. He was clearly in the throes of shock. I swam to him and flipped him face up in the water. As I curled my arm under his left armpit, Wham! I was hit from below. This time my legs were straight down the hippo's throat, his jaws engulfing my legs not quite up to my groin, but much too close all the same.

Evans slipped from my grasp as the hippo yanked me under water. My oxygen-starved lungs burned and heaved. Oh shit, not again.

Now my legs were trapped and my hands were free, and I remembered my gun, the .357 Magnum strapped to my waist. I reached toward my crotch to grab the pistol – like most river guides, I had painted the casing of the bullets with nail polish to keep them waterproof and able to fire when wet – but the hippo was shaking me back and forth so violently that I couldn't grasp the handle.

He whipped me about underwater until I was disoriented. The only sound was the swishing of my body through the water as the hippo thrashed from side to side, up and down, ten feet below the surface. My brain crackled and my lungs strained with the panic of suffocation. Suddenly, everything stopped. The river pig let me go.

Surfacing, I gasped for air and swiveled my head left, then right. No Evans. Ben or Mac must have rescued him by now. I had to get to the rock, get away from this enraged animal. Stroking toward the nearest rock, still 20 yards away, I was amazed that I could even swim. And I was swimming like Tarzan on amphetamines. I knew my body was damaged, but I felt nothing, just every adrenaline-flooded cell screaming to get the hell out of here.

Just a few more yards to the rock. I could see the clients on the other rock outcropping. They were safe. The water to my right erupted. I looked over mid-stroke as the hippo arched through the air like a porpoise, jaws agape, teeth and tusks bearing down on me.

He scored a direct hit, driving me underwater while biting into my torso. My legs dangled from one side of his mouth; my arms, head and shoulders from the other. Down we went into the silence of the river, deeper and deeper. I kicked my legs and tried to twist free of the eight-inch teeth piercing my chest and abdomen, squeezing with such pressure that I thought my head would pop. I scratched at his eyes and punched his bristled snout. He started thrashing about again, and I realized that one of his tusks had bored through my chest. I was skewered like a kebab. I held tight to the tusk with my two free hands, trying to keep him from disemboweling me as he thrashed around.

The hippo surfaced. But he wouldn't quit. Enraged, he seemed intent on killing me. He thrashed about, porpoising in and out of the water, shaking me up and down and side to side the whole time. He was going absolutely nuts. He tossed me into the air, where I did a crazy sort of half twist, and then fell back into the hippo's yawning maw, my head and legs again sticking out the sides of his mouth. One of the clients would later say it was like watching a dog shake a rag doll in its teeth, trying to rip it apart.

The hippo caught me and bit down so hard I was certain he had chomped me in half. Apparently a jet of blood spurted from my side about five feet into the air. I still felt no pain, though I could sense that with each violent twist of the hippo's muscular neck he was ripping me limb from limb. But my mind was crystal clear – I was intensely focused on getting away. The crazed hippo thrashed about on the water's surface and I sucked what little air I could as he dunked me in and out of the water. I tried reaching again for my gun and was able to grab it, only to feel the sharp, crushing pressure of hippo teeth on my arm. The gun slipped down his throat, joining my hat, lucky sunglasses and left sandal.

The thrashing stopped and the hippo dove for deep water. All of a sudden, everything was still. I stopped struggling and tried to assess the situation.

We were on the bottom of the Zambezi, the hippo standing on the river bed with my mangled body clenched in his jaws. I wondered who could hold their breath the longest.

I'm not sure how long we sat there on the river bottom – time passes very slowly in the jaws of a submerged hippo. My blood mingled with the water flowing past. The pressure of suffocation squeezed my chest and throat.

Then he rocketed toward the surface, me in his mouth. The hippo leapt from the water and, still ascending, flung me through the air with a great shake of his head. I landed five yards from a small rock, about six feet wide. I tried to swim but my left arm wouldn't work. "Damn it," I thought, "I'm not giving up." No way was I going to survive the onslaught of this psychotic hippo from hell only to drown a few feet from safety. With the very last ounce of energy left in my body, I stroked toward the rock.

Then, the front of Mac's red plastic kayak appeared inches from my face. Demonstrating exceptional bravery, he risked his life to save mine. I grabbed the boat's nose with my right hand and held on while Mac pulled up to the rock then dragged me up out of the water.

That I made it to the rock was something of a surprise. Equally surprising was the fact that I felt no pain, not even a twinge of discomfort, and I was thinking clearly. I knew this because my next thought was for the safety of Evans and my clients.

I sat up, looked across the water at the bodies standing motionless on the other rock 30 yards away, and counted – one, two, three, four, five, six. They were all there. But my canoe was nowhere to be seen. The hippo had capsized it when he pulled me in, and while I had most unwillingly diverted the animal's attention, Ben had rescued the Germans from the water.

"Everybody stay right where you are," I yelled. "Everything is going to be OK . . . Let's just stay calm. We'll be out of here just now."

The clients remained still, not saying a word, just staring at me. Mac, on the rock next to me, and Ben, sitting in his canoe, were staring also.

"Where's Evans?" I asked.

Ben sat there, his eyes not moving from me. I looked at Mac. "Where's Evans?" I demanded, louder this time.

"He's gone, mate …. He's gone." Mac said. He waited for the words to register. "He went under about 50 yards downstream."

"Shit," I muttered.

My mind launched into crisis mode. "Assess the situation. One person lost, maybe badly torn up, maybe dead. Have to search for him downstream. Six clients stranded on a rock in the middle of the river; a deranged and extremely pissed-off hippo who may or may not be done throwing a temper tantrum. Take control of the situation. You're still in charge, and your people are still in danger. First priority – get the clients to safety. No, wait; assess your injuries first."

I looked down at myself.

"Oh shit."

I was a shredded, bloody mess. My torso was punched full of holes, blood streaming down me onto the rock and turning the water red. My flesh was torn and ragged everywhere. My left foot looked especially bad, as if someone had tried to beat a hole through it with a hammer. I tried to raise my left arm, but couldn't. Up to that point I felt no pain. Then, like a child who scrapes his knee but doesn't think to cry until he sees the blood, a shockwave of pain exploded inside me. I crumpled to the rock.

"Paul!" Mac shouted, crouching down next to me.

The pain had stunned me but now adrenaline flowed through my veins like floodwaters through a gorge, keeping me fully awake and focused.

"Mac," I said, as calmly and authoritatively as I could, "here's what we're going to do." I was thinking out loud, hoping to keep everyone calm while I tried to figure out the next move. Lying on the rock, I raised my head and looked down at myself. I still didn't know exactly what my injuries were, or how much I could expect of my body. Hell, I wasn't sure if I could stand up.

I looked at my left arm. My shirtsleeve, still rolled up above my elbow, was in tatters. Most of the meat had been stripped from my arm; I could see the upper and lower arm bones, cracked and splintered. I tried again to raise the arm, straining to get it to twitch or move. Nothing. I tried to wiggle my fingers. The arm lay there, as still and lifeless as a corpse. Panic percolated down in my gut; my brain was a beehive, a million thoughts buzzing louder and louder. "Where's the hippo? Where's Evans? How am I going to get the clients to shore? What the fuck is wrong with my arm?"

Then my head went quiet, and a single thought emerged: I'm going to lose it. I'm going to lose my arm.

The panic flared, welling up from my stomach to my throat, ballooning inside my head. This was exactly what I couldn't do – fall apart. I was the lead guide, and it was my responsibility to get us out of this situation.

In my head, I heard the voice of my Guiding mentor, Dean McGregor. "Stop thinking about it. NOW! Get yourself together and deal with the problem in front of you. Get the clients and your team to safety. Make a decision."

"Mac," I said quietly. "Pull my sleeve down and cover this arm." Mac gingerly unrolled the tattered fabric and buttoned the sleeve around my wrist.

Taking action was good. My river guide training was kicking in, overriding the panic instinct. I was in control again. Well, reasonably in control, given that I'd just been up to my arse in a hippo's gullet. The hippo had spindled, folded and mutilated me with a savagery unheard of for his species. I was now stranded in the middle of the Zambezi River, and the sociopath hippo might still be nearby.

I scanned the river. Of the dozen or so hippo heads bobbing in place in the water, I picked him out immediately. He was still there, his head occasionally poking above the water, eyeing us just as impassively as the other, better behaved hippos, but giving the distinct impression of brainstorming what he could do for an encore.

"Where's the radio?" I asked sharply.

"Gone," Ben answered. "It was in your boat."

"Damn," I hissed through gritted teeth. "What about the first aid kit?" As I asked the question, I knew the answer – the first aid kit had been in my boat, too. Both the radio and first aid kit were kept in our Pelican cases. As I sat there contemplating my lot in life, the two things that would be most helpful to me right then were probably going over Victoria Falls, safely tucked away in their protective cases.

I tried to curse again. "God…" but instead of spitting out the word "damn", my throat gurgled; I spit blood. I couldn't catch my breath and my breathing was raspy and bubbly in my throat. More blood was filling my mouth. Where was the blood coming from? My mouth? My throat? … My lungs!

"Mac," I sputtered, barely able to get the words out, "sucking chest wound."

Even though Mac and Ben hadn't logged many hours on the river, they each knew the basics of first aid. In the safari world, the basics include knowing how to treat tension pneumothorax – a sucking chest wound. This particular medical scenario arises when the chest cavity has been punctured, say, by a hippo tusk. Inside the chest cavity, the lungs are kept inflated by the opposition of pressures inside and outside the lung. When the chest cavity – or lung, for that matter – is punctured, air pressure is lost and the lung collapses, producing a sucking effect.

In lieu of a surgeon being on hand, the collapsed lung issue can be temporarily addressed by sealing or patching the wound with a non-porous, impermeable material, such as cellophane wrap.

Mac threw open the cooler in Ben's canoe and tore the plastic wrap from a plate of snacks. He pulled off his brand new safari shirt, crouched next to me and wiped the blood from my chest, trying to find the perforation wound. "I don't think it's any of these," he said. "Roll over, maybe it's your back."

Five holes perforated my back and Mac quickly found the suction from the one that was sunk through to my chest cavity. "Here it is," he said, "this one below the shoulder blade."

Tossing the shirt aside, Mac pulled the plastic wrap taut between clenched fists, holding it in front of him like a pillow he was about to smother me with. He pressed the clear film down over the hole and held it there. After a few seconds, I could breathe again. Mac let go of the saran wrap lung patch. Tearing his shirt into strips, Mac applied tourniquets to the more obvious wounds on my limbs, trying to stem the blood loss.

I sat up and looked over at the clients. Marc, Nathalie, Jochem and his wife Gundie, were still standing, frozen with anxiety and carefully eyeing the water around them. Pierre and Murielle were sitting, his arm around her as she sobbed.

I was as patched up as I was going to get sitting on a rock in the middle of a river. I needed to find Evans and I needed to initiate a rescue for my clients. We couldn't wait for somebody else to save us; we had to act now. We were about a five-minute paddle from the shore landing where the forest green Land Rover would be waiting to transport us all back to town.

"Mac," I said, "Stay here with the clients. Ben, load me into your canoe and let's follow the current. We'll look for Evans on the way to the landing spot."

I wasn't too crazy about this idea; in fact, I was terrified of giving the hippo another shot at me. I looked to where his head had been bobbing.

He wasn't there. Or was he? Was he hiding beneath the surface, waiting to finish the job?

I looked at Ben, fully expecting him to tell me that he was very sorry for my current state of mutilation, but with all due respect I could just fuck off if I thought he was ever going to paddle a boat in this river again, let alone right here, right now, with that demonic hippo still lurking.

Ben looked me right in the eyes, as if searching for something. I held his gaze. Taking a deep breath, he muttered something quietly and helped me into the canoe.

Then time froze. The world and everything in it stopped, giving me a minute to look down on this surreal scene. It was twilight, the most gorgeous time of day in Africa when the sun sinks into the horizon like a ball of molten gold. Old African hands say that one never tires of the African sunset, and I wondered if I would ever see another. I realized that I could very possibly be about to die. My wounds were certainly severe enough. And if my chomped insides and massive blood loss didn't do me in, it seemed certain that the hippo was going to give it another go as he seemed to be on a personal mission to see to it that I not leave this river alive.

Time unfroze. Mac was crouched next to the canoe, talking to me as I came back from my time warp.

"Mac, keep everybody calm," I said. "We'll have the rescue team out here as quickly as we can."

"No worries," said Mac.

"And Mac?" I said, in a tone that I wanted to be solemn but not too dramatic, "please tell my family and Jess that I'm sorry and that I loved them."

"Nah," he replied. "You tell 'em yourself, mate."

I lay down with my head propped up on a seat cushion in the middle of the canoe, my feet in the bow. Ben picked up his paddle and sat in the rear. Mac pushed us off into the current.

"Just paddle smooth and easy, Ben. Keep your eyes open, we're gonna find Evans. We're all gonna be OK. Just hang in there."

I was whistling while walking past the graveyard at night, trying to keep both Ben and myself calm, but there was no need; Ben was performing like a seasoned pro, paddling strongly and smoothly while his eyes darted from side to side, scanning the water's surface for Evans and the hippo. He was so completely focused that I don't think he heard a word I said.

Mac shouted across the water to the clients, explaining what was going on. When he finished, the only sound to be heard was the river's muffled hiss and the pig-like grunts of the hippos all around us. Blood was pooling on the bottom of the canoe and sloshing in rhythm to Ben's frenzied paddle strokes. I lay there, silent now, looking at the sky above and trying not to think about what lurked in the river below. Neither Ben nor I said a word, but we both were thinking the same thing – the psycho hippo could be right beneath us. The only thing between his teeth and our arses would be the half inch-thick fiberglass canoe bottom.

Time slowed to an agonizing crawl. It felt as if Ben were paddling through molasses, each stroke seeming to go in slow motion. The anxiety about the hippo, beneath us somewhere, eyeing us, waiting for his moment, was excruciating. But even worse now was the pain. It was so intense that I feared I might pass out – or worse, I might not. Had I not experienced it myself, I would not have believed that the human body could experience such pain. It wouldn't let up, and it was becoming too much. I didn't want to lose it, not now, not in front of Ben, but the pain and the fear of dying was growing every second.

Then suddenly, the pain stopped. In an instant, my body went from a cauldron of hot poison to … nothing. The pain was gone completely. I actually felt good, even euphoric. My eyelids grew heavy. I smiled at the departure of pain and grew even sleepier, overcome by a warm, soothing sense of well-being and peace. I was dying.

"This is it," I thought. "My time is up. This is what it's like to die." As my eyes closed, seemingly in slow motion, I thought I heard the voice of my two year old niece, Nicole … "Uncle Paul" … "Uncle Paul."

Then, things snapped back into focus. I knew at that moment, as certainly as I've ever known anything in my life, that if I went to sleep, I would never wake up. It was that clear – I knew I would die. And I also knew, with absolute clarity and certainty that I had a choice in the matter – escape the pain, easily, effortlessly, simply by slipping quietly into sleep, or choose to live. The choice was clear, clearer than anything in my life before or since that day.

I knew that to live I needed the pain, but I knew I couldn't endure the pain alone. I've never been a very religious person. I always believed in God, but to that point, I lived my life pretty much however the hell I had felt like. But I was familiar with one passage from the Bible that I had come across years earlier when I was working on a farm in Israel, picking tomatoes. It was Psalm 121.

"I lift up my eyes towards the hills, from whence commeth my help?
My help comes from you Lord, you who made heaven and earth,
You will not allow my foot to slip, surely you'll not slumber
Behold you Lord, the keeper of Israel, you'll neither slumber nor sleep
You Lord, you are my keeper, you are my shade at my right hand,
The sun shall not smite me by day, nor the moon by night,
Lord you'll keep me from all harm; you'll preserve my soul,
Lord you'll shield my going out and my coming in
From this time forth and even forever more."

I forced my eyes open, as wide as I could, and the pain rushed in. Agony gripped every cell in my body. Blood sloshed around the canoe bottom; I couldn't believe all that blood was mine. How much more could I have left in me? But in spite of all this – the pain, the traumatic damage to my body, the blood loss – I knew that I wasn't alone. I knew with absolute, unshakable certainty that I was going to live.

We approached the shore where six porters waited at the designated pick-up spot, standing around the Land Rover. These were guys I had trained and who had worked with me for years. Ben yelled over my shoulder, "Kura midza ... vuka iwe!"

Though Ben and all the porters were fluent in English, Ben reverted to the local dialect in the excitement of the moment. What he said, loosely translated, was "Get off your arses and get over here... I need your help now!"

I lifted my head to see over the canoe's bow. The porters rushed into the shallows, pulled the canoe to shore and lifted my broken body out, setting me down on terra firma.

In the half hour or so since the hippo had torn me apart, I'd lost a lot of blood. Had the blood continued to spill while the porters loaded me into the Land Rover then drove five miles through the bush to Victoria Falls Hospital, there's little question I would have died before a doctor ever laid eyes on me. But in what turned out to be a stroke of life-saving good luck, while the hippo was behaving in a most un-herbivore-like manner, the Medical Air Rescue Service, or MARS team, was conducting training drills in the bush just four miles from the shore landing spot. Stan, my foreman, knew this, and radioed the MARS team. Within minutes of Ben and me hitting shore, a doctor and four paramedics were stanching my wounds, keeping me alive for at least a little bit longer.

So there I was, in a small clearing on the shore of the Zambezi. Victoria Falls a quarter-mile away roared like a jet plane on perpetual take-off. I was surrounded by six of my crew, four paramedics, a doctor and Ben. I was conscious, horribly so, and kept mumbling pathetically for someone to give me a painkiller. There was a lot of shouting going on, and it seemed to me that a lot of hands were poking and prodding, wrapping tourniquets on my arms, legs and head. I kept mumbling that I needed something for the pain, but no one seemed to be listening.

I closed my eyes, trying to block out the pain. After another minute of poking, prodding and chaotic yelling, things quieted down. Dr. Nyoni, a trauma specialist from Vic Falls Hospital who had been training with the MARS team was bent over, his face inches from mine.

"Paul!" He shouted. "Can you hear me? Paul, Paul … it's Dr. Nyoni. Can you hear me?"

Slowly, I opened my eyes. I looked at Nyoni. In a halting quiet voice, just above a whisper, I said, "I hear you, Doc. Can you hear me?"

"Yes, yes I can hear you, Paul."

"Doc," I continued in a solemn voice, "there's something I must tell you."

"What is it, Paul?"

"Give me some fucking painkiller!" I screamed. Or at least tried to scream. It came out as more of a forceful whisper. "I need something for the pain NOW!"

Nyoni assured me that he'd give me something "as soon as we get to the hospital," and returned to his poking and prodding. I closed my eyes again, trying to blot out the pain that was increasing exponentially due to my little fit of anger.

Nyoni barked some orders. The MARS team scooped me up, placed me on a stretcher and loaded me into the ambulance. It took ten agonizing minutes for the ambulance to bump and toss its way through the bush, speed along the main road that led into town, and finally pull up to the entrance of tiny Victoria Falls Hospital. The MARS team pulled my stretcher from the ambulance and a nurse took it from there, wheeling me through the corridor.

Looking up, I saw the nurse's upside down face as she zig-zagged my gurney through the dozen or so other gurneys parked along the hallway walls past the bodies that littered the floor. She was carrying on a conversation and it took a few seconds to realize she was talking to me.

"We are very busy right now because of the malaria epidemic," she said, in the casual tone of voice one uses when discussing the weather. "But this is not a problem for you, Mr. Templer. We are taking you through right away."

I wanted to express my gratitude for being taken ahead of the mosquito bite victims, but the pain stopped me short. Seconds after I was wheeled into the operating room, Dr. Nyoni appeared next to my stretcher.

I knew Nyoni well. All the river guides in Vic Falls knew him as he was a trauma specialist, and trauma injuries were a fact of life in Vic Falls. Getting tossed from a raft into churning whitewater is like being dropped into a blender … cracked bones, twisted and sprained ligaments, concussions, head wounds and near drownings are the usual results. On safari, ankles twist and snap, snakes bite, and campfires burn the careless and intoxicated with alarming regularity. Animal-inflicted wounds are not altogether uncommon emergency room fare in Zimbabwe – a goring by a Cape buffalo, the occasional lion attack – but the prolonged assault I'd just experienced was unheard of, and I suspected that my injuries were far beyond the purview of Vic Falls Hospital.

Dr. Nyoni examined me beneath the overhead light. "Paul," he said, "we can stabilize you here and stop the bleeding, but then we must get you to a surgeon."

Only an orthopedic surgeon would be able to determine the full extent of my injuries, but Nyoni knew this much – the hippo had carved at least 38 serious wounds in my body. His tusks had drilled five fist-sized holes through my torso, at least three of them so deep that they pierced my chest cavity; my lung could be seen through one of the holes in my back. Both of my armpits had been ripped open, the axillary artery in my left arm severed. My left foot and ankle were crushed and torn, my Achilles tendon nearly cut in two, and a golf ball-sized hole ran clear through the top of the foot down through to the sole.

Several bite wounds lacerated my neck and head and the right side of my face was split open. One of the hippo's teeth penetrated the back of my neck, just below the skull. This is where the medulla is located, the part of the brain that controls such involuntary functions as heartbeat and respiration. Had he bitten a fraction of an inch deeper, the power flowing from my brain's command center would have been cut off and I'd have died within seconds.

Then there was my left arm. I didn't need a doctor's report to know that it was seriously damaged, maybe beyond saving. And I'm glad I didn't see the doctor's report, which noted a severed brachial artery and described the arm as "degloved from shoulder to wrist."

The nearest hospital with an orthopedic surgeon was in Bulawayo, 280 miles away. It's a little over an hour trip by air, the usual method for transporting severe trauma victims out of the Falls. But air transport was out of the question in this case; because of my damaged chest cavity, the air pressure change inside an ascending airplane would have quickly collapsed my lung. Nyoni arranged for an ambulance.

The MARS team prepped me for the ride, applying more tourniquets and clamps and pumping me full of an electrolyte-laced I.V. I asked over and over about Evans and the clients. Nyoni came to my side.

"Doc," I whispered, "I need to know if they found Evans. Are the clients OK?"

"Your clients are safe, Paul. A motor boat went out and brought them in from the river. They're all fine. No one was injured."

"What about Evans?" I asked.

Nyoni hesitated. "They're still searching for him," he said quietly.

Denial is a powerful defense mechanism, but my reserves were rapidly depleting. I was already fighting off thoughts of losing my arm, trying to block out the picture of me sitting pathetically in a home for the handicapped wearing one of those hospital gowns that wouldn't quite cover my backside while a nurse spoon-fed me. Now the guilt battalion was charging in. What if Evans is dead? What could I have done differently? Why am I alive and Evans …?

After 30 minutes of wrapping my broken and torn parts as best he could, Nyoni removed his surgical gloves and stepped back from my stretcher. "OK, Paul, let's get you to Bulawayo."

"Wait a minute!" I implored, my voice rising with each word. "The pain is getting worse – you've got to give me something for the pain."

"We've already given you morphine," replied Nyoni.

"Well it wasn't nearly enough!" I screamed. This little outburst ignited another spasm of paralyzing agony. I couldn't move; it was too painful.

I didn't know it then, but Nyoni, the nurses and the MARS guys were lying. They were not going to give me anything for the pain – no morphine, no Demerol, no Vicodin or Percodan – not even an aspirin. Because of the damage to my head and neck, they needed me to remain conscious and awake so that they could monitor my condition. It was a long ride to Bulawayo.

The ambulance sped through the inky blackness of the African night. Glyn, a good friend of mine who happened to own the local pizza restaurant, was at the wheel. Nyoni rode in back with me.

For the first time in hours, it was quiet; no water splashing, no people screaming, no hippos grunting. All I heard were tires whining over asphalt as we sped across the African plain.

I thought of my mutilated left arm. When I had directed Mac to pull down my sleeve and cover the arm, it was with a calm acceptance that the arm was gone, that it would be coming off. But somehow, adrenaline, optimism, panic and that built-in human defense mechanism of being able to twist something horrible into something less horrible all conspired in my mind to produce the thought, "Yes, I'm going to lose my arm. Then it will heal and grow back, or be replaced with another arm, just as good, and my life will go on uninterrupted; I will still be a whole person."

But reality was asserting itself. The facts were trickling into my consciousness a little at a time, in manageable doses. My future – days, weeks and months from now – was coming into focus and it didn't include a left arm. This wasn't a torn fingernail. If the arm came off, it wasn't growing back.

"Doc, tell me something," I said, trying to frame my question so as to give the greatest amount of leeway for a hopeful answer. "My arm … I'm going to lose it, aren't I?"

I was fishing. I dropped the tough, hardened exterior of the river guide, almost as a ploy. Part of me felt that if I let on that I was scared, and even acted a bit pathetic, Nyoni would have an opening to give me the answer I wanted.

I knew Nyoni was a tough old bird. He'd spent much of his life in or near the bush and was tempered by the trials and hardships of Africa. I desperately wanted him to tell me, "For God's sake man, pull yourself together. You're not going to lose your arm. It's only scratched up a bit. Quit being a baby."

But in the van's overhead light, Nyoni looked back at me, his gaze unflinching. "Paul, you're alive," was all he said. I asked no more questions.

At 12:20 a.m., about eight hours after the hippo had first inhaled me, I was being wheeled down a hallway of Mater Dei Hospital in Bulawayo. Nurses and attendants hovered around me, surrounded by the garish white of ceiling lights. The rubber tires of the stretcher squeaked along the tile floor and everything passed by with a surreal, dreamlike whoosh.

A nurse's voice shattered the dream. "Before the doctor can see you, sir, we will need your insurance information."

I was about to unload a string of curses on her and her descendants but Nyoni intervened, assuring the air-headed nurse in gentle tones that he would get the information faxed from Vic Falls right away.

I came to a stop beneath a large overhead spotlight. I was in the operating room. Lying there, all I could see was the light above me, and on the edges of my peripheral vision, a collection of stainless steel machines sprouting black hoses and cords. I couldn't see anyone, but they were there; I heard them.

"He's in bad shape ... vital signs weak ... left arm gone ... right arm and left leg probably coming off as well ... not sure he'll survive the surgery."

Now, I knew that I was going to survive. I knew it with every fiber of my being, even if the doctors and nurses didn't. But all this talk of arms and legs coming off was scaring the hell out of me. I thought about trying to make a run for it.

"Hello Paul. My name is Dr. Ncube."

I looked intently into his eyes, trying to establish some personal connection, trying to make him see that this was a real person he was dealing with, hoping that we'd become instant friends and he would be more careful or do something extra to ensure that I'd be okay. Ncube gazed back at me just as intently.

"Hey Doc," I said, "I know that you're gonna do what you've gotta do ..."

Still looking me directly in the eye, Ncube calmly interrupted. "I won't know the extent of your injuries until I've cleaned the wounds. There is serious damage to both of your arms and your left foot, but I don't yet know how serious."

He looked at my arm, then back at me. "The left arm is very bad, Paul. I will save as much of it as I can."

The nurses gathered around the operating table, manning their stations. The show was about to begin and I wasn't going to be around for it. Though Ncube and the nurses thought this was all about keeping me alive and saving my life, I knew that wasn't the issue. I was going to live. The question was, with how many limbs?

"Hey, Doc," I said, as a nurse helped Ncube with his surgical mask.

"Yes, Paul."

"Let's take the minimalist approach, huh?"

Ncube's eyes peered back at me from between his surgical mask and the cap pulled down over his forehead. He looked as if he was considering my request, and nodded. The sedatives snuck up from behind and whacked me over the head like a velvet club. I was out, finally free of the pain.

Ncube pulled on a pair of goggles. He reached over to a stainless steel tray, picked up a surgical saw fitted with an eight-inch, stainless steel circular blade, and cut off my arm.

Chapter 5

Waking Up in My New World

March 1996
Hospital

I woke up staring at the ceiling. For five minutes I stayed that way, just staring up. I didn't want to look down. I didn't want to see which body parts were still attached and which were gone. I wanted to stay just as I was, staring at whitewashed nothingness, surrounded by the warm, post-surgical fog.

I started to explore my body with my mind. It felt as if everything was intact. Maybe there had been no amputations; maybe even my left arm was still there. Still staring at the ceiling, I wiggled the fingers of my left hand. I could feel them move. They were still there!

The joy and hope and excitement were too much and I rolled my head to the left to look at my wiggling fingers and saw... nothing. I kept wiggling them. I could feel them move. But in the space below my elbow where my forearm, hand and fingers should have been, there was nothing but empty space. The fingers that I could feel drumming on the cool white bed sheet were phantoms. My left arm had been amputated above the elbow.

Not moving my eyes from the white of the bed sheet alongside my torso, I could taste the panic rising up through my throat. Now that I knew I couldn't rely on my sensory perception, my sense of physical feeling, the existence of every other part of my body was in question. It felt like I still had a right arm and two legs, but did I?

I rolled my head to the right.

Yes! Not only was my entire right arm still attached, I could move it, too.

Next I looked at the sheet that covered the cage that kept the bed linen off what I hoped were both of my legs. Noticing that I was awake, the nurse came over to me. It turns out that she was a veteran intensive care unit nurse; she'd been taking care of really messed up people for a really long time. As she stood by my side I could see that she understood exactly what was going on here. It was weird; it was as if she could read my mind. It was as if she knew that I really didn't want to look, that I was too scared to see… but at the same time that I needed to know what was left of me.

Without a word passing between us, she leaned over me and whipped back the sheet. I looked. There at the bottom of each leg was a foot. Each had five puffy little pink toes. Granted, the one foot was really mangled, but the bottom line was that both of my feet were still attached to me.

One limb gone, three still attached and in working order. What a relief. There was some odd psychology at work here. Rather than despairing over the fact that I had lost a limb, I was hugely relieved that I had lost only one limb. In my post-operative, narcotic haze, the numbers seemed pretty good. Three out of four was not bad.

I lay there with a doped-up smile, thanking God. I was quite satisfied with my seventy-five percent success rate. Then, the drugs descended on the stage of my mind like a heavy curtain, fading my world to black.

It would be a long time before I ever again considered myself fortunate or believed that I had come out ahead in my encounter with the hippo.

For the next twenty-four hours I was in and out of consciousness. I was trying to keep my head above the surface but was getting yanked back down, over and over by the undertow of sedatives coursing through my body. I don't remember much, other than two conversations, one with Ncube, and one with my Mum.

A few hours after waking up and realizing I'd lost an arm, I woke again to see Ncube pulling a chair up next to my bed.

"I saved as much of your left arm as I could, Paul." We both looked at the raw stump of flesh extending from my shoulder, the end of it cross-hatched with blue surgical stitches. "We will have to watch closely to make sure no infection or gangrene develops in what remains of your arm."

The joy and gratitude I had felt at losing only one limb had diminished considerably. In fact, I was now pretty pissed off and feeling very sorry for myself.

Ncube continued. "Paul, you are extremely lucky to be alive. This hippo that took your arm, he also saved your life. It is clear that you were not meant to die."

I said not a word.

"You should have suffocated from a collapsed lung. But the hippo's tusk pierced the chest cavity in such a way that, rather than creating a hole, it created a flap of skin. The flap of skin closed like a valve, sealing the chest cavity and allowing you to keep breathing."

Mildly interesting, I thought, but lucky?

"The hippo also severed the brachial artery in your left arm. Blood loss from such an injury typically leads quickly to death. But in your case, the hippo's tooth cut at an angle. It's as if the artery were a piece of spaghetti with a thin, hollow center. Somehow, the hippo's tooth pinched the artery shut. It sealed itself like a piece of cooked spaghetti."

Turning my head slowly to the left, I looked at the empty space below my left bicep. Just as slowly, I turned back again to look blankly at Ncube. The dramatic effect I was going for was, "You've got to do better than that."

The surgeon stood up. "It could have been much worse, Paul," Ncube said.

"How could this be worse?" I demanded.

Ncube reached into the pocket of his white surgical coat and pulled out … my underwear. He held the garment up, dangling it between his thumb and index finger. I immediately recognized the little blue and white striped number as the pair I had been wearing when the hippo attacked me.

With his other thumb and forefinger, Ncube grabbed the other side of the waistband and held the briefs up so that I could see the front – the business end, if you will. The underwear was made of two-ply cotton, and the front of it was torn, but only through the first layer of material. The hippo's tooth had ripped down through the outer layer of material, but left the inner layer – and all that had been behind it – unscathed.

He had me there. Things most definitely could be worse.

Ncube then spoke the words that will remain etched upon my mind until the day I die.

"Paul, I have cut off your arm. You have two options – you can lie back and feel sorry for yourself, or you can get on with your life. It's up to you."

He got up to leave. "I'll be back to check on you in a few hours. In the meantime, think about what I have said."

For the next two days, I continued to go in and out of consciousness – mostly out – due to the high octane painkillers and sedatives pumping through my veins. All that I remember of those two days is the pain, the angry self-pity and the conversation I kept trying to have with Mum.

Mum had flown from Harare to Bulawayo Sunday morning after a long night of frantic phone calls back and forth with the MARS office, Mater Dei Hospital in Bulawayo, and her friends Ron and Norma Barker. It was Ron and Norma who had picked her up at the airport that morning and had the unenviable task of delivering the "good news-bad news" scenario to her. Her only son was alive, but his arm had been amputated and he was far from being out of the woods. Some time Sunday afternoon, I awoke to find Mum standing next to my bed. The sniveling commenced immediately. Not from her, from me.

Mum's a tough woman. Any woman who lives in Africa needs a certain toughness, and in my Mum, Sally, that streak ran as wide and strong as the Zambezi.

Mum and I were always close; I kept few secrets from her. Though she never pretended to like it, she understood my calling to be a river guide. She tolerated it in the hopes that before a Grade 5 rapid pinned me against a submerged rock, or an irritated elephant swatted me to a pulp with his trunk, I would outgrow my adolescent fascination with danger and adventure, and get "a proper job".

But her patience wore out. Six months prior to the hippo incident, Mum and Stewart, my stepfather, came to Victoria Falls for a week's holiday and I took them out on our own private safari. It was an excellent trip with tremendous game viewing that included herds of elephants, as well as buffalo, giraffe, zebra, crocs, and of course, hippos. We spent the night in front of the campfire while lions called to each other in the darkness.

Any tourist looking to experience the beauty of Africa would have been thrilled with that overnight trip. But my mother, having seen my work firsthand, became a lot less tolerant of river guiding as a profession. Before returning to Harare, she suggested that if I was at all interested in prolonging her life a few years by minimizing her worry and stress, I would quit river guiding sooner rather than later and find employment that didn't require raving lunacy and a latent death wish.

A few months later, I called her in Harare and said that after five years as a river guide, I'd had my fill of the Zambezi and had quit. I already had new employment; I would spend a season as an apprentice safari hunting guide. After that, I would get a hunting guide license. The sky would be the limit for my little safari consulting company, Carpe Diem Pvt. Ltd.

So when she got the call that I had been chomped by a hippo, Mum thought I was up in the north country with a fellow hunting guide and our trackers, assisting the National Parks Department on a problem animal control mission. A pride of lions were making a nuisance of themselves up there, attacking livestock and villagers. We were to go in and neutralize the problem. But there was a delay, and I was waiting around in Vic Falls, killing time. A fellow guide was struck down by malaria and asked me to cover for him on a canoe safari that Saturday afternoon. I said yes, happy for the chance to be back on the river.

Now here I was, trying to explain this to Mum, telling her that I hadn't lied, I really had quit guiding, and that this wasn't my fault. Mum kept interrupting me. "It's all right, Paul," she said over and over. "You just need to rest now and get better. Stop talking ..."

But I kept trying to convince Mum that this wasn't my fault, and trying to convince both her and myself that I'd be all right. Most of all I was scared, and my Mum was the one person in the world who I would let see me that way. I cried to her like a baby, asking "Why did this happen to me? What the hell kind of life was I going to have now that I was mutilated, less than whole ... now that I was handicapped?"

During one of my interludes of consciousness, Mum told me that my girlfriend, Jess, and my sister, Lisa, wanted to come to the hospital.

"No," I screamed. "I don't want to see anybody. Please don't let anyone in here, Mum. I don't want anybody else to see me like this."

In my mind, what had happened to me was an embarrassment, something shameful. I felt like less than a man. And as far as I was concerned, I was going to stay hidden away in this hospital for the rest of my pathetic, miserable life. I made my Mum promise not to let anyone in, and she agreed... for a while.

The next day, I was a little more lucid and spent the morning talking to Mum, trying to be strong. But I kept falling apart, dissolving into emotional meltdowns that made a bout of PMS seem like a mere blip on the irrationality meter. Around noon, the narcotics caught up to me and dragged me back into the dark, gauzy underworld of unconsciousness.

I woke up around 3 p.m. Mum was walking into the room with a cup of tea she had fetched from the nurses' station. I resumed my only partially coherent babbling about how sorry I was for making her worry, that this wasn't my fault, blah, blah, blah. Then, I noticed the strange look on Mum's face.

"What's wrong?" I asked.

She said nothing, wrinkling her nose as she sniffed the air. Her eyes got wide and for the first time since she had arrived at the hospital, my Mum looked scared. She set her cup of tea down on the table next to my bed. "Just a minute," she said, "I'll be right back." She spun around and left the room.

She returned with three nurses in tow, each of whom immediately got the same look on their face; a wrinkled nose, "What in the hell is that smell?" look. Before I could figure out what was going on, Mum left to find Dr. Ncube. The nurses unwrapped the bandages on my left arm, or rather, my part-arm. They weren't being gentle in the least, and their jostling and yanking hurt like hell. But keeping my mouth shut seemed the wise thing to do. Something serious was afoot.

Ncube walked in, looked at my arm, and instructed a nurse to prepare the operating theater. The room became a blur of activity. "What's wrong? What's going on?" I demanded. But no one paid attention. I couldn't make out what the hell they were talking about, though I heard the term "gas gangrene" more than once.

As the nurses and orderlies lifted me onto a stretcher, the local priest strode briskly into the room. He had been to visit when I first arrived and had administered last rites to me. Whatever had Mum and everybody so excited right now was apparently enough to make the priest think another round of last rites was in order. He then asked if I wanted to make a confession.

"Father, I'm grateful for the opportunity to make good with the bloke upstairs, but I really haven't been able to get up to much trouble since we last spoke."

They wheeled me out of the room past Mum who was standing in the corner out of the way. "You're going to be OK," she said, but the look on her face told me that though she willed it with all of her heart, she didn't believe it.

Somebody clamped a mask over my face before the stretcher even came to rest, and I was unconscious in seconds. My Mum would later tell me that the odor in my room was unlike anything she had ever smelled, but she knew what it was. It was the smell of death.

More specifically, it was the smell of gas gangrene, a bacterial condition that can arise in soft tissue following surgery. In my case, bacteria – perhaps from the Zambezi's water but more likely from the hippo's tooth – had taken up residence in the tattered tissue of my arm, and began rotting my flesh in a very unappetizing process known as putrefaction. The rotting flesh gives off a gas – gas gangrene. If gas gangrene gets into the blood stream, which it inevitably will if not treated, it can go systemic. Once the gaseous bacteria reaches the heart, which takes about seven minutes, the show's over.

I learned all this wonderfully enlightening medical information only after awaking from the emergency surgery. That was when Ncube informed me that he had no choice; the only hope of preventing the gas gangrene from reaching my heart was to cut it off at the source. So that's what Ncube did, firing up his motorized saw once again and slicing my arm off at the shoulder.

Following the gas gangrene amputation, an oxygen mask was clamped to my face around the clock, to flush out any bacteria that might still be lingering. They told me how lucky I was, that the gas gangrene would have killed me if my Mum hadn't walked in and smelled it when she did.

By this point, though, I really couldn't care less about how lucky I was. I spent my time bouncing back and forth between a buoyant, narcotic euphoria and periods of depression and anger that occasionally erupted into cursing, foot-stomping rants. I was slowly coming around to a decidedly superficial level of acceptance regarding the loss of my arm. It was too overwhelming to look at the big picture, the long term implications of what this was going to mean to me and my future. Instead, I focused on little pieces of the picture, such as my phantom arm.

It's typical for the brain of an amputee to continue to act as if the now missing limb is still there. The neuron pathways in and out of the brain are so well worn from years of use that impulses still flow from the brain to where the limb is supposed to be. One of my early experiences of the phantom funnies was in the hospital when a ferocious itch flared up on my left elbow, a body part which, of course, no longer existed. But the itch existed. It wasn't just something in my head but an actual physical sensation, and it was driving me nuts. To make matters worse, my right arm was still pretty useless; I could barely move it.

Jess and my Mum were in the room and I begged Mum to scratch the itch. She didn't know what to do, but started scratching in the general area of where my arm should have been. It didn't do a thing; the itch got worse.

I became more insistent, telling her "No, not there, higher. No, Mum, you're not doing it right."

I became more and more angry until Mum and Jess couldn't control it any longer. They started giggling. I stared at them, dumbfounded at their egregious breach of political correctness.

Then I giggled. I threw back my head and laughed. For a moment, my attitude was, "Hey, get over it, get on with it." But that attitude was often hard to come by.

The morning routine infuriated me. The nurses would wake me up at the ungodly hour of 6 a.m., putting me in a nasty mood right off the bat. They'd take my temperature, administer my meds, and then leave me for an hour or so before returning to feed me breakfast. I felt like a newborn infant being tended to by a rotating team of nannies. But there wasn't a damn thing I could do about it; for the first couple of weeks it was physically impossible for me to get out of bed, let alone walk. I ate in bed, bathed in bed and pooped in bed.

The drill after breakfast was to change my dressings. The nurses would give me a shot of anesthetic, give it five or ten minutes to kick in, then peel the bandages off my shoulder, clean the wound, and put a new dressing on.

One day, after the nurses had taken off the bandages, they were called away to an emergency in the operating theater. After laying there for a few minutes, I started to get worked up. I rang the bell to the nurses' station. No response. I rang again. Nothing. I held the button down for a minute and then started pounding it with my fist. I screamed for somebody to come and take care of my goddamn arm. No one came. I was vaguely aware that I was still pretty whacked out from my morning cocktail of painkillers and was perhaps being a tad irrational, but … since I was still whacked out from my morning cocktail of painkillers, I didn't care.

"That's it!" I shrieked, veins bulging from my neck. "I'm fucking out of here!" I rolled off the bed and stood unsteadily. I grabbed the portable I.V. hanger next to my bed, to which I was connected via an I.V. tube. I set off down the hall lurching along like a drunken, howling Frankenstein, my body a patchwork of stitched flesh, purple scars and bloody wounds. Of course, as I had no left shoulder to speak of, my hospital gown kept slipping down which added just the right amount of "insane asylum escapee" flair to my comportment.

"You people are bloody useless!" I screamed down the empty corridor. "I'm leaving this God-forsaken shit hole!"

And I meant it. I was going to cross the lobby, walk through the double doors, and set off down the road to Harare – 300 miles away. I unleashed a string of semi-coherent curses on the entire Mater Dei hospital staff, informing them that I was leaving and nobody had better try and stop me.

In my self-obsessed rage, I didn't notice the figure coming toward me from the other end of the hall, at a brisk pace. When I did notice, I still couldn't make out who it was through my rage-blurred vision, but it didn't matter – doctor, nurse, security guard, policeman – whoever it was, they were about to experience the wrath of a very angry and doped up amputee if they didn't stand aside.

The approaching figure and I were on a collision course which it seemed determined to maintain. I bellowed, and was preparing to smite the interloper with my I.V. hanger, when a flash of recognition stopped me.

"Oh. Hi Mum."

The look on her face told me that my great escape was over – right now. She gently turned me around and led me back to my room, letting me know in a soft but firm voice that hippo attack or not, there was no excuse for boorish behavior, and it'd be a good idea to stop acting like a jackass and let the nurses do their job.

She put me to bed, whereupon the injection of several doses of sedatives precluded any more wandering that day.

I don't want to give the impression that I was a complete arse all of the time that I was in the hospital – I wasn't. But I did have my moments.

One of the nurses was a little old Catholic nun, Sister Agnes. She stopped in one afternoon just to see how I was doing, and I quickly and in no uncertain terms informed her that I was not doing well at all, and that it was all her boss' fault. Not the hospital administrator boss, but the big boss.

She then had the audacity … the temerity … the unmitigated gall … to respond serenely:

"Your situation, Paul, though perhaps unfortunate and not at all something you had planned for, is what it is. It is now a fact of your existence. You have the opportunity to grow through the experience, or not. You have choices. How your life will unfold from this point on is up to you."

She pointed out that "her boss" had jumped in and given me a hand when I needed it. She was just getting into her "It's all part of life's rich tapestry, thy will be done" spiel when I told her I'd had enough, and using language I'm not at all proud to have used, told her to leave the room and to take her loving boss with her.

For several days after the two amputations, I continued to insist, rather unsuccessfully, that I didn't want visitors. But my Mum decided she knew better – which she did – and after I'd been in the hospital a while, a steady stream of friends and relatives filed in and out of my room.

Jess, my girlfriend, was amazing! I was afraid she'd find me repulsive or pathetic. I was afraid she'd feel obligated to stay with me because now I was an amputee, while at the same time I was deathly afraid that she'd leave me for the very same reason. But she was incredible. From the minute she walked into my room and smiled at me, she never once looked away or showed even the slightest sign of disgust or pity and she supported me in every way.

Though I regularly spilled my guts to Jess and my Mum, I adopted a hard-arsed, upbeat posture in front of everybody else. I laughed and joked with family and friends and some guy who I didn't know but was kind enough to come and visit me; he lost his lower right arm when he walked too close to a lion. When several friends from the guiding fraternity visited with a smuggled bottle of whiskey that, judging by their bloodshot eyes, was left over from the night before, I snuck a few swigs while they took hits from my oxygen tank to quiet their throbbing hangovers.

To everybody but Mum and Jess, I put up the front. "Yes, I'm OK, a bad day at the office but these things happen." I think I fooled most of the people, including myself, into believing that I was really okay, that I was dealing with the loss of my arm bravely and without self-pity. But Mum, Jess and I knew the real story. I was scared, angry and had no idea what I was going to do with what was left of me and my life once I got out of the hospital.

Meanwhile, I had become something of a media star. Newspaper and TV reporters from all over the world who were in Zimbabwe to cover the presidential elections stumbled upon a sensational human interest story – not quite "man bites dog," but "hippo eats man" would surely interest some readers. The press flocked to tiny Mater Dei Hospital, begging Mum and the front desk for an interview or at least a photo. I wasn't interested, and the hospital staff was vigilant in allowing no one near my room who I didn't know. But one afternoon a photographer somehow snuck into my room and snapped a picture while I was sleeping. A week or two later a photo that managed to make me look in even worse shape than I actually was graced the pages of tabloids around the world.

When I wasn't impressing visitors with my false stoicism and good-humored tough-guy routine, I watched TV. Mum and Jess brought videos of Super 12 Rugby, a sort of world championship featuring the best dozen teams of the southern hemisphere. I had played rugby growing up and was a pretty decent player. I watched the Super 12 teams for hours on end, immersing myself in the games and temporarily forgetting that I was confined to a hospital for the short-term and to the pathetic life of a handicapped person for the long-term.

But TV watching could also be hazardous to my emotional stability. A friend dropped off a video of the sexy HBO series, *Red Shoe Diaries*. For the first few minutes, I was as engrossed and hormonally-hyped as any normal, healthy young male would be when watching soft-core erotica. But in the middle of a particularly steamy scene, I suddenly remembered that I wasn't normal. I was deformed, messed up and less than whole.

"Who are you kidding?" said the voice in my head. "No woman is going to be interested in a handicapped amputee. Don't even think about it. No woman's going to ever love you, and you sure as hell aren't going to get laid ever again."

I grabbed the remote control and turned off the TV. Ten minutes of wallowing silently in self-pity made me feel worse and I turned the TV back on and flipped through the channels.

A commercial showed several smiling, laughing people splashing around in a pool and others jumping in to join them. I freaked out. I don't know what happened exactly, but the splashing water transported me back into the jaws of the hippo, thrashing about in the river. He was dunking me over and over and I couldn't breathe; he kept biting into me, breaking my bones, popping my internal organs, and ripping off one limb after another. It was like it was actually happening all over again, and though part of me knew it couldn't be happening, I couldn't break free from the terrifying flashback.

I'm not sure how long this lasted, probably just a few minutes. When the panic finally subsided, I reached to the side of the bed and buzzed for a nurse.

"Yes, Paul," said Sister Agnes as she walked in, in a sweet and caring voice that harbored no trace of resentment for the appalling behavior I'd exhibited in our earlier conversation. "Is there something I can do for you?"

"Yes, please Sister, there is," I said, in a contrite tone that bordered on pleading. "Could you sit with me for awhile and watch Super 12 Rugby?"

She smiled. For the next three hours Sister Agnes, with her royal blue and white nun's habit, rosary beads and faith enough for two, sat with me and watched some of the southern hemisphere's finest beat the hell out of each other on the rugby field.

The doctors operated on me twice more, both times performing skin grafts to seal the holes in my left shoulder, right armpit and left foot. Perhaps my memory was blunted by time, or maybe by the mind's need to diminish traumatic experiences, but the pain from the skin grafts made the hippo injuries seem like a stubbed toe.

The hippo had left only two areas of my body unscathed – my groin and right thigh. These were literally the only parts of me that weren't sore. But the doctors fixed that, making all of me sore by harvesting the unscarred skin from my thigh to graft onto the wounds. The indescribably painful procedure involved dragging a cheese grater-like tool down my thigh and peeling off a thick, fleshy strip of epidermis, leaving the skin like raw meat with a million exposed nerve endings.

As the end of my month-long hospital stay drew near, I was less and less able to adopt my upbeat, things-will-work-out posture and was increasingly prone to anger, fear and depression. They had recovered Evans' body, and the autopsy showed he had drowned, without a mark on him from the hippo. The guilt was at times unbearable, and was like gasoline on the fire of my already antagonistic stance toward God. If he wanted to screw my life up that was one thing, but why did he have to kill Evans, too? I knew there was nothing I could have done on the river that day to prevent what happened. It wasn't my fault. But this intellectual understanding did nothing whatsoever to alleviate the emotional burden that weighed on me night and day.

The prospect of leaving the protective cocoon of the hospital to face the real world scared the hell out of me.

The night before I was to be discharged, Mum's friends, Ron and Norma, paid a visit, along with Jess. They pushed my wheelchair out onto the hospital's veranda and we watched the sunset, sipping gin and tonics. We laughed a lot, got a little drunk, and Ron and I discussed me getting out on a golf course pretty soon.

But friends and gin weren't the only reason for my good mood. That afternoon, a letter came from my close friend and guiding mentor, Dean McGregor. It wasn't unusual that Dean hadn't visited me; he's a different breed, most comfortable guiding clients on safari or simply disappearing into the bush by himself for days at a time, and not at all comfortable with such societal trappings as enclosed buildings, cars, traffic, or shoes.

Dean and I and a few others in our circle of guides had talked for years of doing the first full descent of the Zambezi River – kayaking her from source to sea. It was our shared dream.

Dean's letter was typically brief, but filled me with a hope that I was afraid had been lost forever, carried away in the waters of the Zambezi:

Boetman: Shame about your arm.

We may not be able to paddle the full Zambezi, but we can still walk her.

Dean

Coming Out of the Hospital . . . The Darkness

Coming out of the hospital was interesting. I thought that I was doing a pretty good job of dealing with my lot in life. With the benefit of hindsight, I was in fact living in denial and drinking a lot. I was, for a while anyway, the poster boy for the "Woe is me" club. Trying to look back rationally at all that had transpired, I kept coming back to the same old questions.

"What if I'd taken a different route? Why didn't I see the hippo? Why was I there in the first place?"

To the priests and nuns and any other folks who dared to offer me "Thy will be done. It's all part of life's rich tapestry... ", I'm more than a little embarrassed to admit that I was pretty darned revolting. At the time, I felt that I had proof that this loving God concept was a giant lie. After all, how could some entity that supposedly loved me, subject me, my family and friends to all we were going through? And then, to prove what an ego trip he was on, he went ahead and took Evans' life on top of it! So then my survivor guilt came up with questions like "Why had I lived and he died? Could I have done more to save him?"

After a particularly vehement outburst one night, Mum did the smart thing. She convinced me to go and see a shrink, not that I needed to see one of course, but maybe he could help me get everyone else off my back.

During the first couple of sessions, I spent the bulk of the time telling him how cool I was and how well I was handling it all. I was fine, and it was all the others who were messed up. Then my real feelings began to surface. I talked about how my nearest and dearest didn't understand what I was going through or how I was feeling. They didn't understand what it was like to be an incomplete person, to lose my self-image, my identity and my sense of worth. They couldn't understand the questions I dealt with, like how could I provide for a family? How could anyone ever bear to be with me to consider having a family? I was going to grow old alone. I might as well go and join a freak show.

I spent a lot of time at my own private pity party. I couldn't even begin to comprehend how anyone could want to be with me, that anyone could look at me and see anything other than a grotesquely mutilated lump of flesh that used to be Paul. In my eyes, they were with me because they felt sorry for me. It was some sense of obligation that kept them around. Not only was I trapped in this ugly new world, but so were those who had been a part of my life before.

A testament to my family and to Jess, they all stuck with me through thick and thin. No matter how hard I tried to push them away, no matter how scared I got, no matter how angry I got, no matter how much I hurt them, they stuck with me.

Drinking seemed to be the one way that I could escape my reality. Finding solace in a bottle, I'd become the consummate egomaniac with an inferiority complex. I couldn't stand myself. I felt incomplete, less than whole, and less than human. If I couldn't stand myself, how could I possibly expect anyone else to? But after a few drinks, I could begin to believe that I was the man that my nearest and dearest and the press made me out to be, that I'd done all that I could do to save Evans, that what had happened was just a fact of my life. I could wear my disfigurement as some sort of twisted badge of honor. Sitting at the bar, I'd be normal, even interesting at first. Then, as the drinks flowed, I'd become obnoxious and pathetic before Jess, or whoever happened to be on duty, would pour me into a car and take me home.

I was convinced that my cat Solo was the only one in the world who didn't see me any differently. The first time I saw him, I was lying down in quite a lot of pain and he just came and snuggled up where there once had been an arm, looking at me with eyes that conveyed that unconditional love that pets seem to so freely give. That look, that acceptance, I was convinced was now reserved to animals, and no person would ever look at me again without pity.

As I worked with the shrink, my world and the relationships in it evolved. Jess and I grew closer, in a platonic way. She became one of my few constants as she helped nurture and nurse me back to strength.

Subconsciously, I'm pretty sure that we both knew that too much water had flowed under the bridge for there ever to be any kind of romantic relationship, but she'd see me through to the next stage, whatever that might be.

On the drinking front, I once asked the shrink if he thought that I had a drinking problem. "I'm not going to say you do or that you don't, Paul. What I can offer is that you have a maturity/thinking problem." Hearing what I wanted to from that conversation, I breathed a sigh of relief and took it that drinking wasn't a problem.

Cleared to travel, the next port of call for treatment was to be England if I was going to realize my dream and get a prosthesis that was going to make me whole again. Medical bills and not working for a while meant that finances were tight and it was only through the goodness and support of family, friends and acquaintances that somehow the trip and getting fitted for a prosthesis became a reality. I can still feel the frustration and anger at the thought that finances were all that was standing between me and getting fitted with the device. I thought the device would address a lot of the psychological issues I was dealing with, as well as the practical ones.

One particular blow, when counting the pennies, was the small print in one of the insurance policies I carried. It spelt out that if I "knowingly and willingly put myself in danger/at risk" it would negate the policy. Learning this, some dear friends in the safari industry, Wayne and Muffy, threw together a well attended fundraising dinner, part of the proceeds going to me, and the remainder going to Evans' family. Mum's group, the Soroptomists, put together a fundraising golf outing. The state lottery donated funds, and British Airways donated tickets.

Jess and I were off to London and before long, I was being fitted for a prosthesis. Some friends hired me to help with their English based safari company, Safari Drive. I wasn't much use around the office, but they kept me on, taught me how to use a computer and began the process of rebuilding my self-esteem.

My prosthetic arm was taking longer than we'd envisaged and I decided to get a part-time evening job, something near our apartment. It was then that I got a firsthand experience at what being handicapped was going to mean in other people's eyes. It wasn't like I was looking for work as a surgeon or anything that required a high level of dexterity. I'd walk the high street and there'd be notices in the windows of bars and stores saying "Help wanted". I'd go in and inquire and once they saw that I was handicapped, I'd be told "Sorry, that position has been filled" only to see it still advertised days later. I got pissed. I decided upon a new strategy.

"Hi, I've come in to see about the job you have advertised in the window." I inquired at the party store counter. "Sure, let me call the manager," the counter assistant offered. Clasping eyes on me, I could see the cogs turning in the manager's mind as he walked towards me.

"I believe that you're here about the vacancy," he started. "I'm sorry, but it's been filled."

Before he could continue I challenged, "Look, I appreciate your concerns, but how about you give me a chance. I'll work through the end of the week for no pay. If I can do the job, then hire me with back pay. If not, I walk away. You've got nothing to lose." He went for it.

That night, Jess and I celebrated. As a former safari guide and owner of my own consulting company and builder of others, I'd secured employment as a shelf stocker.

Six months later, I left that job and England. I had an arm, but it wasn't the fix-all that I'd imagined it would be. Jess and I were still together. We'd learned a lot about each other and about life. I was far richer for the experience, largely thanks to Jess. Back home in Zimbabwe, I got a job working the customer service department for a computer company. I had an apartment, a car that didn't need four-wheel drive and I was miserable. If this was what life was going to be, I wasn't sure that I wanted any part of it.

One night, Jess and I went to see "Fiddler on the Roof". While we were at the theatre, Jess gave me a phone number in America and suggested that I call it that night. She didn't say much more.

Into the Light . . .

"Hi, my name's Paul Templer. I was given this number to call," I told the voice at the other end of the line.

"Paul, thanks for calling," the enthused voice responded. "I was recently at a wedding reception in England and sitting next to me was Henri, a friend of yours. She told me your story and I'd like to fly you to LA next week. I'm producing a show for Fox called *When Animals Attack*, and I'd like to feature your story."

A couple of conversations later, Mac and I were on an airplane bound for the U.S., not before taking leave from my job and chatting over a few beers with my close friend and mentor, Dean.

I'd served my apprenticeship as a safari guide under Dean. Along the way, we'd become firm friends. Zimbabwe's answer to the Marlboro man, Dean was the Madison Man. Appearing on the big screen merely accentuated the fact that Dean was in fact larger than life, a consummate bushman and true friend. Reminiscing about how, whilst I was in the hospital, I received the letter from him regarding our dream to explore the Zambezi River, we agreed that I'd seek out funding and support so that we might realize our dream. I was all too ready to go for it. Why not?

Mac and I had a great time in LA. It wasn't just that we were away from home in a new world. It wasn't just a couple of guys having fun. We were having an absolute blast meeting new and fascinating beautiful people, our egos getting pumped up at every corner, our every whim catered to. It was the intangible, inexplicable excitement that came from the surety that we were embarking upon a yet undefined new adventure. It was the feeling that you get in the pit of your stomach when something is afoot. Faced with the prospect of leaving that most uncomfortable of places, the comfort zone, we jumped in with both feet, exposing ourselves fearlessly to whatever the future might hold.

Fox got their interviews and we entered into conversation with an independent production company who professed an interest in working with us to realize the Zambezi dream. An added bonus for me was that Fox agreed to route my ticket home via Michigan so that I could renew my acquaintance with some old friends who had got back in touch with me after reading about my bad day at the office in their local newspaper, the Detroit Free Press and later on in Reader's Digest.

Aware of my dissatisfaction regarding my prosthetic arm, they'd, unbeknownst to me, taken it upon themselves to organize a fundraiser to get me a new arm. I arrived in Detroit to a series of TV, radio and newspaper interviews and a fundraiser. An old friend, Patty, was spearheading the effort. As we were leaving Patty's house to go to the fundraiser, the phone rang. The chap on the other end of the phone told Patty that he represented a Prosthetic company, Wright and Filippis. He said that they'd heard about my plight and would be happy to meet with me the following week. Life was happening and it was happening fast.

The fundraiser was a great success. I was deeply touched by the generosity of people, their best wishes, the notes of support and kind words, not to mention the cheques that arrived in the post. It was all quite overwhelming.

As Patty and I sat nervously in the conference room along with Doctor Ray, a friend, waiting for the team from Wright and Filippis to come forward, I couldn't help but wonder at how my life continued to spiral out of control. It was surpassing my wildest dreams. Then, I got blown away even more.

We'd gone through the initial conversation with the prosthesis people, introducing ourselves and establishing my circumstances. Then, they explained what could be done for me with two comments that changed my life forever. The first was from Rob, my prosthetist.

"Paul, what you have there is a paperweight. I can make you an arm."

Not wanting to get ahead of myself, and all too aware of the financial reality of my situation, it was the words and actions of Ken Woodward and Tony Filippis, two of the greatest men I have ever met, that overwhelmed me with joy.

Ken said, "Paul, don't worry about the money. We can work that out. No one should ever have to go without a prosthesis because they can't afford it."

Days later, I severed the umbilical cord with my past. I called Jess to let her know that I'd be staying on in America for a while, ostensibly to get my new arm and the therapy that went with it. Then, I called the company that I'd been working for to let them know that I wouldn't be back.

Chapter 6

The Expedition

ZZAM
Spring 1997

O ver the next few months I became totally self-absorbed in looking out for myself. I got my new arm and I learned how to use it. I also started to learn what it meant to be handicapped. I learned that I had choices, that I could be miserable and handicapped, feeling sorry for myself, or I could be happy and handicapped, living whatever life I wanted to live. I also began to realize that I could be useful and that I had a voice to be heard.

I reveled in the publicity I received. As an amputee who happened to arrive at this place through somewhat exotic circumstances, I had the unique opportunity, and with that, the responsibility to do something good. More and more, my thoughts and empathy went to those tens of thousands of kids who lived in war-torn countries like Mozambique and Angola who, on a daily basis, were stepping on landmines and losing limbs. I had to do something.

What began as a mere pipe dream evolved into a raison d'etre. The production company I'd been working with in California agreed and the ZZAM expedition began to take shape. The skeleton plan was that I would lead a team and canoe from the source of the Zambezi River to the ocean, which had never been done before. We would use this trip as a vehicle to realize my new dream, which was to spread the word about the dangers of landmines and raise awareness about the plight of their victims. I wanted to do something to help these sufferers, to be a part of the solution that one day there might not be any more new victims. Throwing myself at this proved to be somewhat cathartic; using what had happened to me to help others exorcised some of my demons along the way.

Just before I left the U.S., I met an American chap at dinner who was to be vacationing in Africa in the not too distant future. His name was Dave Williams and we hit it off. We agreed to meet up for dinner when he was in Africa.

Arriving back in Zimbabwe, I had to face the reality of the new life I'd chosen. First things first, I had to resolve the Jess situation. One of my biggest regrets from that time is the way I treated Jess. So far as being a partner in a relationship, I certainly didn't keep up my end. While in the States, I'd sent the occasional email narrating a series of events, which usually was the extent of the conversation. She deserved a lot more than that. Having stood by me and supported me through thick and thin, she deserved so much more than I had or was willing or able to give her. We arrived at the amicable realization over a surprisingly civilized cup of coffee that we were done. It was time to get on with our lives independently as we were heading in very different directions.

I'd sucked her dry, taking everything she had to offer and giving little in return. Driving away that night, I really didn't think that it was over between us. Fate would somehow bring us back together. The weeks and months that lay ahead saw me trying to manipulate the situation such that I could have my cake and eat it too. Fortunately for both of us, she was a lot stronger than I was and we were done.

Shortly thereafter, the relationship that I'd built with the Californians fell apart. As life would have it, a couple of days later I met with Dave, the American, for dinner.

Dave is an incredible man; a sailor, a fine food and wine aficionado, a successful entrepreneur and a caring human being. He is an inherently good man who believes wholeheartedly that life is what you make it and that morality and hard work are the measure of a man. Dave not only talked the talk, he walked the walk.

We shared a particularly fine dinner during which we discussed at length what was going on in my life and then parted ways. A couple of days later, sitting at home in my apartment, my phone rang. It was Dave.

"Paul, I've been thinking about what we talked about and I'm committed to making it happen." The dream had a new lease on life. We discussed what needed to happen next. I committed to spend the next few weeks putting together a detailed, well grounded plan, and he committed to meet with me in Detroit where we'd start to make it happen.

I came up with a plan and after tapping friends and family for financial support, supplemented by an investment from Dave, I came up with the money necessary to put that plan into action. Part of the research included identifying and learning about existing programs that supported landmine victims. We had no desire to reinvent the wheel. Our contribution would be to identify existing programs that we felt compelled to support, and then support them.

A milestone moment occurred. I was in a Maputo, Mozambique meeting with Max Deneu, who ran the POWER program. POWER is a British based organization that helps provide limbs to victims of landmines. Max Deneu was showing me around his facility, introducing me to people in the government and giving me insight into how things worked.

The exposure to the reality of the situation left me with no doubt that I'd found my calling in life. Arriving at his facility, I was overcome with gratitude at my lot in life. Sure I was an amputee, and that sucked, but my God, I had it so much better than any of the people I was to come into contact with. These were the forgotten, ignored innocents of our world, collateral damage and casualties of war. These were the men, women and children who we all heard about on the TV and radio or read about in newspapers and magazines. They were mothers who had stepped on landmines while fetching firewood and the children who'd been blown up whilst reaching for some shiny object they found lying on the ground.

Hope for the Future

If I had any doubts about what I was involved in, they diminished in one profound instant, prompted by my encounter with a very special woman. She stood poised, her tatty garments hanging loosely from her body and her children crying and staring off into space. Protruding from her dress, next to her badly scarred remaining leg was the prosthesis that Max had made for her. It wasn't the kind you'd see in the developed world, but it was a practical, functional blend of plastic and a metal pipe with a brown rubber foot attached. Our eyes locked. She took a deep breath and raised the lump of metal and plastic that was attached to her stump and took her first tentative step. What happened next was one of the most touching, meaningful experiences I've ever been privy to.

I witnessed a smile that changed my life forever. It was a smile that illuminated her future and my own. A smile of realization, not only that she had a functioning prosthesis, but that she had her life back. It was an amplification of the smile that I smiled in the luxurious surroundings of the conference room in Michigan when I first received my prosthetic arm. Looking at her smile, I felt humility like never before. I realized that I had a faint inclination of what she was experiencing. I had empathy for what she was going through. I could not compare, but I could identify with what she felt. Her smile signaled lifting despair.

Only moments before, she'd perceived her life to be one of abject poverty with children she couldn't support. She now had a shot at life. She wouldn't be the subject of media attention. She wouldn't earn fame and fortune and accolades, but she could return to her village to once again fetch firewood, work in the fields, and support her family by scratching out a living. She and her family now had a shot at survival.

Making the Dream a Reality

Armed with the requisite information and driven by the inherent belief that I had found my calling, I bid my family and friends adieu and boarded the airplane that was to take me to Michigan to meet with Dave and my future. We worked as if we were possessed to come up with a plan. It was quite simple. I was to lead my team on the ZZAM expedition which was to serve as the vehicle to launch Make-A-Difference, the nonprofit corporation whose declared objective was to spread the word about the evil of landmines, to raise awareness about the victims they create, and to be part of the solution, that one day, there would be no more victims.

One of the first things I needed to do was to put together a team that would have a shot at realizing this impossible dream. I asked Andy, Dean and Max to help me select our team. We spent many long nights figuring out who would come. The long list had been whittled down to eleven. It hadn't been easy. Not only were there requisite skills that needed to be brought to the team, but equally important was the need for the individuals to be able to work as a team and endure everything that lay ahead. The mix of personalities was as important, if not more important, than the skills they brought. Ten of the eleven knew each other well, had worked together for years and trusted each other implicitly. The eleventh was my call and my responsibility. The lads didn't like it, but they trusted me that I knew what I was doing.

The most important role was that of logistical back up. The man selected was Rory, my brother-in-law. He was going to have the toughest job of all. In the extremely unlikely event that things went smoothly, he was to see to it that we were re-supplied when needed and that we got in and got out in one piece. In reality, he was to be our salvation when things went wrong, and we knew things would go wrong. If someone was injured or killed, he needed to get the body out. If things went to hell, he needed to come up with a plan to get us back on course. A daunting task when you consider that we were to be in the middle of nowhere, with no conventional means of support for much of the time.

The ten who were going to be on the water had the easier task. We were to get in, enjoy the experience of a lifetime and then get out in one piece. Of the ten remaining, nine of us were accomplished bushmen, having spent years working on and around the Zambezi River, all had an intimate relationship with Nyami-Nyami, the river god, and a reverence for her domain.

First, there was Dean, bushman extraordinaire and expert river guide. Andy possessed the same skills but, where Dean was a free spirit, Andy was incredibly organized. A former member of the illustrious British Parachute Regiment, his leadership and discipline would be invaluable. Max, as well as being an accomplished river guide, had been working for MineTech, a mine clearing organization. Since much of the area we were traveling through was littered with landmines, he was an important ingredient to the success of the venture.

Of the nine, Dave Carson (Dave C.) was the least experienced on the river, but an expert bushman. His real strength to the team was his ability to get along with and to bring out the best in people, to make them laugh and to help them keep things in perspective. I knew that we'd need his sense of humor to pull us through the tough times. James Boardman (Red), an expert kayaker, bushman and my personal rock of Gibraltar, was as loyal a friend and colleague as any man could ask for. Barry, an experienced river guide and paramedic was our medic. Batch, the lone South African on the team was an accomplished outdoor cameraman and would film the expedition. Dave Humpleby (Dave H.), my longtime expedition buddy, whitewater madman, back-up medic and photographer would shoot stills.

This brought me to number ten. I needed a journalist, someone who would report on the trip as it progressed; filing stories, updating the website and then at the end, produce materials that would publicize the expedition to illustrate what Make-A-Difference stood for. Additionally, number ten would work with me at the end of the expedition writing a book that would tell our story and generate further publicity for our cause. I met Chris, a journalist working for a well-established American media organization. And though he didn't know the first thing about kayaking, Africa or the great outdoors, we'd established a rapport and a degree of trust. I felt sure that he was our man, so using my declarative power as leader, I made him number ten. I had my team.

With the team in place, the logistics were next. While Max, Dean, Andy and I had come up with what we needed, making our wish list a reality was a mammoth task. Dave Williams was more than up to it. Seeking corporate sponsorship was obviously the ideal, but given the timeframe, we were unsuccessful. Every day we waited, more people were getting blown up and suffering. The ZZAM Expedition was the launch vehicle for us to reach our long-term objective, and given that it was November and the water levels would be at the ideal level in April, we didn't have much time to seek out sponsorship, secure publicity, or gather all the necessary equipment.

Dave Williams decided to finance the operation out of his own pocket. It was going to cost a fortune to do it properly and Dave and I agreed that there was no point in doing it if we didn't do it properly. The costs started adding up – the team salaries, the boats, cameras, laptops, firearms, insurance, logistical backup, and food. The list seemed never-ending. Dave was so committed to helping those less fortunate than he, that to this day, not a single cent ever donated to Make-A-Difference has gone to recouping any of the costs that Dave covered for the expedition.

All the while, I was in America. Metro Detroit had become the epicenter of our mission. I was working with Dave to promote our venture, deal with logistics and build a relationship with Chris, preparing him as best I could, for what lay ahead. One night, Chris invited me to join him at a local bar for a few beers, to meet his siblings.

Carrie

Woodys, the local bar where we met, was packed that night. "Great," I thought to myself, "This is all I need, to spend a night in a crowded bar making small talk with people I don't know."

Realizing that it was quite important that I get to meet Chris' family, I sucked it up, put a smile on my face and fought my way to the bar. I'd met Chris' sister Julie before and spotted her chatting to a bloke, who based on the resemblance, the dark hair, his face and lithe body, had to be Jim, Chris' brother. They were chatting to this stunning blonde. I quickly reevaluated the situation and came to the conclusion "Hmmmm, this might not be so bad after all."

"Hey Paul, this is my brother Jim and my sister Carrie." Julie made the introductions. I was taken aback. Not only was the blonde Chris's sister, but she was even cuter than I'd first thought.

She was tall, at 5'10" with an athlete's body, the face of a hazel-eyed angel and dirty blonde locks which complimented the air of supreme confidence she exuded. Carrie, it turned out, had recently returned to Michigan, having spent the last few years at university on a basketball scholarship studying to become a nurse. There was something inexplicable going on, some kind of undeniable connection between us. We all ended up closing the bar together before Carrie and I took our leave of the rest of the group and ended up watching the sunrise over a cup of tea at a little all night diner.

We spent that night as if we'd known each other all of our lives, at the same time, delighting in discovering one another. We shared our hopes, our dreams, our fears and our lives. That morning when she dropped me off, I was giddy with excitement. My heart soared, I'd met the one, but then my head took over, this was neither the time nor the place. There was no room in my life for this right now and even if there was, she was an American and I lived on the other side of the world. So much for logic. As my head hit the pillow, I remember smiling. I knew I'd met my soul mate.

The days and weeks that followed sped by in a blur. By day, I worked with Dave getting Make-A-Difference and ZZAM on track. By night, Carrie would pick me up at midnight after her shift at the hospital, and we'd both go and get a beer or something to eat and talk. After about a month of this, one of our friends informed us that tongues were wagging as Carrie and I were spending every available moment together, yet we both assured anyone who'd ask that nothing was going on. That night, sitting in a hot tub, we laughed at everybody's interest and concerns, and we gave them something to talk about. Let the practicalities be damned, we were in love. The details would work themselves out. Before I left for ZZAM, I gave Carrie a diamond along with the declaration that I loved her and notice that should I survive the expedition, I wanted to spend the rest of my life with her.

Last Preparations

Preparing for the expedition turned out to be more of an ordeal than I'd envisaged. Having devoted so much time and energy to getting the pieces in place, I'd been able to ignore many of my fears. My nonchalance in interviews regarding risking my life and limbs belied my true concerns. As far as the team I'd put together being the most competent group ever assembled for this undertaking, I had no doubt. But for as much as we could plan, there was more that we couldn't. As the leader, I knew that I needed to "Serve to Lead" as the Royal Military Academy at Sandhurst's motto attested. My men's well being, safety and survival were ultimately my responsibility as was the success of the ZZAM Expedition.

A part of me wanted to lead the expedition as proof that disabled doesn't mean unable. Yet, in moments of complete honesty, I knew that as the leader, I was hiding from my disability under the full beam of the spotlight. I was scared that my ego might be putting myself and others needlessly at risk. I wondered if my disability was going to unnecessarily expose some or all of my team to danger. At the same time, I had a deep rooted belief that I was the man for the job and that I had to do it.

My friends thought I was nuts. When the reality of the adventure dawned upon them, a few of them sat down with me at different times and shared that they thought I was being selfish and stupid and that I needed to start dealing with my lot in life in a way that wasn't so fraught with danger. Besides, hadn't my family suffered enough? How could I put them through this! And what about Carrie?

Ironically, my family and Carrie were my biggest supporters. Not that they wouldn't have preferred I didn't do it, but they all realized that for me to get on with my life, I needed to do it. There were demons I needed to exorcise and realities I needed to face. This is what I needed to do, and God willing, it would all end well. I would come out the other side, not only older and wiser, but at peace with myself, my world and my place in it. In short, they saw that I had to do it and supported me in my endeavor. I haven't the words to express the love and gratitude that I felt for their support. I'm pretty sure that I couldn't and probably wouldn't have done it without them.

So why was I doing this? This was not only a question that I asked myself time and time again, but one that I was asked by most everyone who knew and loved me. I had my standard answer, "Because it's there to be done."

But there was so much more to it than that. Though plenty of people had tried to do it, to date, no one had succeeded. There weren't many things left to do in this world that haven't been done. I had lost an arm, but to me, that just made things more interesting. When Rob, my prosthetist made me a paddle that we strapped to my remaining arm allowing me to paddle a boat again, I knew that paddling the river from source to sea was something that I could do. In fact, it was something I had to do. But in the brief moments when I was honest with myself, I acknowledged that I was doing it for another reason. I knew that it gave me a few more months before I had to deal with the reality of my life without my arm.

It would be very dangerous, but I was so self absorbed and scared of actually facing the reality of my new amputee life, I'd usually offer some macho response along the lines of, "It wouldn't be an adventure without some danger, would it?"

It was much more to me than a boy's adventure or an opportunity to avoid dealing with my new lot in life. It also was an opportunity for me to help some people who really needed help rebuilding their lives. So many lives had been shattered in an instant, irreversibly turned upside down by an act of war, a birth abnormality, or some other random act of God. I knew that I had an incredible opportunity to use what had happened to me to help others who'd been fucked by the fickle hand of fate. Hopefully I could inspire some to re-engage in their lives and help them regain some level of independence and dignity.

ZZAM Expedition – Getting the Show on the Road
Spring 1998

The Zambezi River had a full bag of tricks at her disposal. If some of the magnificent stretches of white water didn't get us, then there were hippos, crocodiles, lions, buffalo, elephants, poisonous snakes, spiders, scorpions, malaria-filled mosquitoes, sleeping sickness, landmines, terrorists, freedom fighters and warlords. Sure, it was dangerous but I had every confidence in myself and in my teammates that we could do it.

The expedition equipment arrived in Zimbabwe and it was time for me to bring the team together, get things started and make the dream happen.

The Yank journalist's plane touched down at Harare International Airport beneath the sweltering midday sun. I was nervous as I stood there waiting for Chris to pass through immigration. None of my teammates were all that excited about Chris joining our team and most of them had made that abundantly clear. It wasn't just the thought of being stuck with a city slicker American journalist who they thought they had very little in common with that bothered them; it had more to do with his complete lack of outdoor experience, and they labeled him a liability. They thought of him as a potential danger to himself, to the rest of our team and to the successful completion of the mission.

I let it ride – they had every reason to be concerned. If he ended up doing something stupid and hurting himself, it could slow us down or even put an end to the mission. Worse yet, when he messed up – because we all knew that as a rookie he would – we'd be the ones who'd have to rescue him and quite possibly pay for his mistakes.

However, I needed someone with Chris's skill set on the team. I was confident that if he survived long enough, then the lads would come to see that they had more in common with him than they had at first thought. Journalistic skills aside, I had a strong sense about Chris's personality. The way he looked at the world and his very different life experiences were going to contribute to the richness of our journey. He would enable us to see and appreciate more than our familiarity would allow. The lads didn't like it, but they accepted it.

Chris didn't help matters much as he walked towards us. There we were, sun bronzed and for the most part, pictures of health, milling around casually in our shorts, t-shirts and sandals. Then there was Chris, his pasty skin the color of the snow he'd recently left behind, sweating like a man on his way to be hanged, in his navy blue sport coat, white long-sleeved shirt, pressed khaki pants and dress shoes. If ever there was a fish out of water, it was him. Nonetheless, I was glad to see him and as I introduced him to the lads, they politely shook his hand and without a word passing between them, each made it clear that the clock was ticking and that Chris was going to have to prove himself soon. I wasn't planning on losing much sleep over it. I knew that in the short term, even if they didn't like him, they'd look after him.

The first leg of our adventure involved eight of us piling into a Toyota Land Cruiser and heading off into Mozambique for a few days. I planned the trip this way for a few reasons. First off, I wanted the team to start gelling. Next, I wanted to introduce Chris to the Africa that he was going to be spending the next few months in. It was not the stuff of tourist brochures or popular fiction. We were going to be immersed in an Africa that few would visit by choice.

I also needed to handle the business side of things. Given that landmines and their victims were central to our mission, I needed Batch to get some film footage of a mine clearing team at work, Dave to take some photographs and Chris to start filing stories. This way we could test all of our fancy new equipment and test the process we'd designed for communicating and coordinating with our bases in Zimbabwe and the U.S.

Mozambique was still one of the most heavily land-mined areas in the world and we were heading off to one of the most heavily land-mined areas in Mozambique. We were going to a village on the banks of the Zambezi River called Tambara. Max's company had a team there clearing mines and they were expecting us.

The journey in was unremarkable, so long as you weren't viewing it through Chris's eyes. With each passing mile, it seemed that the distance between his cubicle at the newspaper office in Detroit and our vehicle was amplified. He was particularly taken with the AIDS awareness billboards on the side of the road featuring a young woman sitting on a young man's lap, advising passersby, "Don't leave home without a condom." Then there were the ubiquitous red backed signs adorned with the skull and crossbones and large letters spelling out "PERIGO MINAS" which means "Danger, Mines". These signs seemed quite relevant as we bounced along mile after mile of dirt road punctuated by the odd crater marking where some poor sod had hit a mine.

Having spent much of the last year in Mozambique clearing land-mines for the family firm MineTech, Max's familiarity with the local customs and his functional command of the Portuguese language were turning out to be huge assets. We drove hour after hour with nothing on either side of the road except vast stretches of thick, waist-high bush interrupted by the occasional village. The villages were usually nothing more than a dozen mud and brick huts with thatched roofs. Mountains loomed along the horizon.

Occasionally we were on asphalt, but more often, we were on dirt. Max had an outdated road map of Mozambique so we stopped from time to time so he could ask people along the road for directions. The jokes we'd made at the beginning of the trip about hoping that Max was better at clearing mines than he'd been at paddling boats didn't seem quite so funny as we bumped along the road. I was incredibly impressed with Max when, at the end of yet another dirt road, we pulled into the MineTech camp.

It was nothing more than a small clearing with seven tents side-by-side and a picnic table beneath a towering tree. On the other side of the tree was a fire pit and a chicken-wire pen caging a half-dozen chickens. We pulled up to the camp and quickly unloaded our gear. It was 2:00 p.m. and we had just four hours until sunset.

Moku, one of the MineTech foremen gave us the guided tour. About a half mile down a beaten track, a MineTech crew was working on "quality assurance". The area they were working on had already been cleared, but it was standard procedure to randomly re-sweep the area to make sure the job was done right the first time. It's not really an "if at first you don't succeed," kind of job. There are no second chances with landmines. Max told a story about another mine clearing company who recently performed a quality-assurance sweep when one of the de-miners stepped on a landmine. As his foreman ran to assist the screaming man whose right leg was blown off below the knee, the foreman also stepped on a mine. Both died.

We watched the team for a while. We were standing at the edge of a shallow ravine cleared of brush and small trees, though a few large trees remained. Seven de-miners, clad in orange-cloth jumpsuits and hard-hats stood abreast at the top of the ravine. Each had several short metal prods and trowels of various sizes in his tool belt. Each carried a metal detector, just like the ones used at beaches around the world to search for buried coins.

The mine clearers stood at strict attention. All were former soldiers in the Zimbabwe Army. All served under Max's dad, Colonel Lionel Dyck, who founded MineTech. The crew leader stood at one end of one line just a few feet from the other seven lanes. Each lane was marked by string stretched taut a few inches off the ground. The strings stretched laser-straight down the ravine and up the far side of the hill.

"Number One, activate your detector."

The man closest to us reached toward his right hip and flipped a switch on a black box the size of a dime store paperback. He snapped to attention.

"Number One, check your detector."

The ex-soldier passed his detector over his spit-shined black, ankle-high military boot.

Suddenly a piercing BEEP, BEEP, BEEP split the air. We recoiled. Max leaned over to me and whispered, "If the detector picks up on the metal eyelets in his boot, he's ready to go."

"Number One, advance."

Number One swept his metal detector slowly back and forth in front of his boots. With the detector continuously shifting from left to right, then right to left, he paused three seconds then eased his left foot forward. He lowered it to the ground and paused again. A minute later, he had covered about five meters.

"Number Two, activate your detector."

"STEP WHERE I STEP..."

The drill began again and proceeded for hours, one man at a time.

Moku turned and motioned for us to follow him back up the path. We fell in behind, single file, but at a greater distance than before. Everybody stepped precisely where the guy in front of him stepped. Moku stopped where the ribbon-lined path turned to the right and spun on his heels to face us. He stopped and looked at the ground. We froze. He motioned us forward.

As we rounded the tree, we nearly stumbled over a human skeleton in the knee-high grass. It was almost intact and looked like one of those skeletons that hangs in a doctor's office, except this one was missing a leg just below the hip. The right femur extended down from the hip, but where the knee should have been, there was only shredded bone.

"It is unusual," Moku told us, "to find skeletal remains of landmine victims. Typically wild animals will take the carcass and eat it, but in Mozambique, the civil war has wiped out most of the wildlife. The animals were either killed for food by roving soldiers, or they died like this person – by stepping on a landmine."

Moku led us through the bush back to the road and towards the village. About 30 meters from a cluster of six mud huts, the ground swept down into a shallow valley. A well-worn footpath wound down the hillside from the huts to the tall, lush grass on the valley floor. The footpath was lined with those tell-tale red-tipped stakes set about a meter apart.

Most of the people of Tambara fled to Malawi to escape the civil war in Mozambique. When they returned to their village, they found it had been heavily mined. Mine fields often go undetected until people are blown up.

MineTech knew the area where we were standing had been mined during the war because a former soldier told them so. MineTech warned the villagers that mines were in the area. Then they cleared a path from the village to the valley floor where the villagers could go for water, firewood and to tend their corn crop.

Tsitsi

For nearly a year, dozens of villagers walked the footpath several times a day. Moku told us a story about one of those villagers, a young twenty-something year old woman named Tsitsi who along with her husband Shadrek and their four young children, lived in a small hut on the east side of the village.

Tsitsi and her family had returned to Tambara once things quieted down. Tambara had been the setting of some hellacious action during the recent civil war. Now that peace was the order of the day, people flooded back to their homes and tried to pick up their lives as best they could. It had been about a year, and life was pretty much back to normal for Tsitsi and her family.

They lived in a mud hut. They were subsistence farmers, scratching out whatever living they could from the land. There were a few rangy chickens running around their hut and Tsitsi and Shadrek spent their time tending their meager maize crop that provided enough food to feed their family and a little extra left over to sell or barter with their neighbors.

Through my eyes it seemed a pretty bleak existence. Tsitsi's day was comprised of going down to the river's edge to fetch the daily water supply and to do the family's washing. While she was there, she would have to avoid getting eaten by the ever-present crocodiles that patrolled the water's edge, waiting for some unsuspecting or careless person to become a meal. When Tsitsi was finished, she would collect firewood to build a fire that provided warmth, protection and a place to cook for her family. The rest of her day was divided between working in the fields with Shadrek, grinding picked maize seed by hand and being a mom.

Moku was working three kilometers away and heard an explosion. "I knew right away what had happened," he said. "We sped to the village, and as we drew closer to the screams, we knew that all was not well."

With the heavy load of firewood atop her shoulder, Tsitsi had stumbled and her right foot landed about eight inches off the path that she'd walked every day for the last year. The force of the explosion launched her body backwards; she landed on the other side of the path on top of another mine. Her left leg, abdomen and right arm were shredded and burnt. It took Moku and his men a while to get to her, but the team of medics saved her life that day.

That was about three weeks prior. Since, she had been taken to a doctor, but no one had heard from her. With little to no communication, no one knew if she'd made it or not. Shadrek and their kids were left to fend for themselves, hoping against better judgment that she'd return. There wasn't much hope as they knew too well that less than half of the people maimed by landmines lived to talk about it, at least in part, because of inadequate medical facilities.

Kids and "Leprosy"

As Moku finished telling us his story, I spotted a gathering of small children beneath a copse of leafy trees. It was the landmine awareness class that I'd been invited to speak to about dealing with adversity.

Moku handed me over to Billy Paul, a MineTech employee who worked in the company's Community Mine Awareness Program. When

MineTech de-mines an area, Billy recruits a couple of locals and teaches them about the dangers of landmines. They then educate the other villagers about the risks.

Though 39, Billy looked no older than 30. He was a former soldier and had worked for MineTech for about five years. His trim, fit physique reminded me of some bantamweight boxers I'd seen in the ring. Dressed in pressed khaki fatigues, a crisp black T-shirt, polished black army boots and a brilliant white baseball hat emblazoned with the orange MineTech logo, Billy was a sharp guy. At odds with his appearance was his crutch clasped tightly under his right arm.

Two years earlier, Billy was working as a de-miner with three other workers. They were working in an area already checked. When Billy lifted a log, his left foot slid about half an inch outside the roped-off safe area, triggering a landmine. His left leg disappeared in a cloud of smoke.

He introduced me to Edina. Edina was an attractive young lady. Though in her early twenties, her eyes belied her age as they conveyed unimaginable suffering, a common affliction in war zones. We shook hands and before long, were chatting animatedly through Billy, supported by my broken Portuguese and her broken English.

Before long, our entire class had assembled. About eighty children between the ages of newly born and ten were completely engaged in the program with me, the strange one-armed man they called "marungu" which means "white man". It was easy to hold their attention as their lives were littered with landmines and constant reminders of those who have inadvertently found them. Our hope was that by educating the children about the dangers of the mines, some of them might be spared the inevitable outcome of their natural childlike inquisitiveness.

Near the end of the class, I was basking in the gratitude of having found something that made my life seem worthwhile. I felt like I was making a difference. I looked across at Edina with the utmost affection and respect. I could see that she was enjoying a similar moment. Maybe we could invent a future here; maybe Make-A-Difference could support her efforts. I wondered out loud what horror had induced her to leave her family to travel around the country doing this incredibly worthwhile work.

"She was forced to leave her village," Billy stated matter of factly. "She has leprosy."

To my dying day, I'll deeply regret my reaction to that news. I couldn't catch my flinch in time as the word "leprosy" battered my senses. In an instant, a multitude of scenarios and reactions coursed through my body and ignorant mind.

I'd lost my benevolent notion of inventing a future with this incredible woman and her cause. We'd shaken hands. Had I caught leprosy? How could God be this cruel, one arm ripped off by the hippo and now the other one was going to drop off with leprosy? How dare she shake my hand? Why wasn't she in a leper colony?

Edina also heard Billy utter the word "leprosy." Watching my reaction, her eyes spoke volumes; she'd been through this before. She looked as sad and as disappointed as anyone I'd ever seen. The mood was gone. She knew it. I knew it. The kids knew it.

As the crowd dispersed I couldn't get away quickly enough to find Dave H., our team's medic. He had to be able to do something. Surely he could clean the leprosy off before it could do whatever it was that leprosy did. I didn't even know what leprosy did and neither did Dave or anyone else on our team. We all shared the ungrounded fear and unanimous consensus that at that moment, it sucked to be me.

Edina slipped away unnoticed.

"Hi honey. What's wrong?" Carrie, my wife to be, a nurse, thousands of miles away in Michigan asked me over the satellite phone.

"What do you know about leprosy?"

To cut a long story short, Carrie told me that I was a fool, that I couldn't catch leprosy by shaking hands and that I needed to find and apologize to Edina for my boorish behavior.

I never did see Edina again and it's extremely unlikely that I ever will. It's too bad – I'd like to thank her for the lesson she unintentionally taught me that day about the costs associated with acting out of ignorance or in response to my knee-jerk reactions. I'd love to give her a hug and apologize to her for being such a fool.

Later that evening, I was concerned that we may have exposed Chris to a little too much of Africa a little too quickly. Washing down a traditional meal of overcooked salty goat meat, maize gruel and some kind of vegetable with a few warm beers, we huddled around the campfire and listened to Chris in his shell-shocked American accent as he described what he'd learned about a recent round of traditional justice.

It seemed that a crocodile had been making something of a nuisance of itself by eating some of the villagers. It was determined by some of the elders that a rather unpopular woman must have cast a spell on the crocodile encouraging it to turn against people she had a gripe with. She denied this accusation vehemently for a few days, but they beat her incessantly until she confessed to casting the spell. Once she'd confessed, everyone knew that the only way to get rid of the spell was to feed the woman to the crocodile, which they promptly did. After they fed her to the crocodile, the villagers had to concede that that the woman may have been telling the truth, since after her death, the attacks hadn't stopped. I was pleased with the way Chris was responding to everything that he was being exposed to. It was clear to me that he was getting an inkling of what he'd signed up for. He was beginning to realize how far away he was from his world in Detroit.

The Team Coming Together

I headed home delighted. Mission accomplished! The guys were bumping into each other, marking their territory and finding ways to work together effectively. Chris now had a pretty clear idea of what we were up to and I was satisfied with the way he'd shown up. He passed his first test with flying colors. On the business side of things, we got some great film footage and photos and had exposed some deficiencies with our equipment. I was concerned about the power supplies for our cameras, laptop computer and satellite phone as the solar panels were not performing the way that the manufacturers had told me they would.

When we finally got back to our base after a few solid days travel, there was a message on my answering machine that the rest of the team was waiting for us at a nearby pub. That night, the Bulldog Pub set a record for beer sales.

At the crack of noon the following day, the first of the collapsed bodies on the floor of my apartment stirred. Two hours later, propped up by gallons of coffee, dozens of fried eggs and pounds of bacon, it was time for us all to get on with what happened next. Max had agreed to serve as Quartermaster; he called us all to order and started handing out parcels. The scene was right out of a Christmas fantasy played out by a group of very excited, overgrown little boys. As Max doled out the gear, each of us unwrapped his bundle as if it were a gift. We each put on our bright yellow life jackets, yellow helmets with miner's headlamps, black and blue sunglasses, sandals, rain ponchos and fleece jackets.

Ten flashlights were switched on and off. Ten river knives were extracted from their sheaths and the blades used to shred cardboard boxes. Ten double-bladed kayak paddles were checked out to make sure that they were the right size and the blades were set correctly.

Zambezi River

Dean ran around impersonating a two hundred plus pound mosquito with a two-foot long proboscis trying to drill through Dave Carson's all-body bug suit while Max posed for a photo wearing every single item in his kit. Everyone was very excited. A half hour later, we all agreed that the kit was awesome, and more importantly, we all looked good wearing it.

We set off to a nearby lakeside safari lodge to do a final test on our equipment and a farewell press conference. Dave Williams had flown in to wish us bon voyage and to meet with Nelson Mandela's future wife, Graca Machel, to discuss the plight of regional landmine victims. At the lodge, we played about with the equipment, showing off to family, friends and the press.

Dave Williams and I spent most of our time chatting with the press, including the folks from *Carte Blanche*, a South African cable TV show that is something like *60 Minutes* but with a softer edge and more of a human interest angle. Airing every Sunday night at 7 p.m., it is apparently the most-watched show in southern Africa. They planned to do three or four segments on the ZZAM Expedition, and would meet up with us at points along the Zambezi.

The one question we were all asked time and time again had to do with how we were handling the dangers of the trip. I, probably better than anybody else, understood the press' preoccupation with danger, violence, mayhem, death and animals gone wild. The mere possibility of danger was exciting and it lured in viewers and listeners and sold copies.

I shared a common understanding of the dangers that lay ahead with my teammates. We understood it the way the race-car driver understands it as he straps on his helmet and fireproof suit. Or the paratrooper as he prepares to leap out of an airplane, or the football player watching his teammate carried off the gridiron on a stretcher, immobilized with a spine-crushing neck injury. We knew the risks, the danger and the chances of being disabled or killed, and frankly, that's what made the expedition exciting.

We shared an incredibly healthy respect, but not a whole lot of fear for that which we knew. This confidence shouldn't be confused with arrogance – between us, the sum of our experiences in responding to challenging situations evoked confidence. We were pretty sure that when the shit hit the fan, we'd respond the way we needed to and our teammates would do the same. We also accepted that anything we couldn't foresee, we would deal with when it happened.

The only real fear we experienced came in dealing with the unknown, and Angola epitomized the unknown. The embers of years of civil strife still burned in the war-ravaged country, threatening to re-ignite at any moment. It was a hellhole teetering on the edge of anarchy. I believe that the wars in the former Portuguese colonies of Mozambique and Angola were the main reasons why no one had successfully paddled the entire river from her source to where she flows into the sea. A group like ours traveling through Angola anytime during the past twenty years would almost certainly have had a pretty tough time and may have been killed. Renegade soldiers, competing warlords, guerillas, bandits, landmines – these were the unknown elements and though none of the interviewers or reporters really honed in on this, it was the element that we all feared the most.

With cameras rolling, microphones tipped towards us as we spoke and reporters scribbling in notepads, we completed the official press conference and then told the reporters that if they had any more questions for the team members, they could ask us at the cocktail party.

The party began. Most of the team's families were there with pride beaming from their faces. Several family members passed their press folders around to the team members getting everyone's autograph.

The cocktail party lasted several hours longer than it was originally scheduled, and after family and friends had gone home, we moved the party into the lodge's bar.

The bar was quiet when we entered with only a young couple from Australia sitting on the bar stools chatting. The bar manager, Brett, had been waiting for us to wander up from the lake. He welcomed us with a round of drinks and offered a toast to a successful, safe trip.

Eleven glasses were raised and drained in unison, and instantly, as if someone flipped a giant power switch to ON, the bar was awash in testosterone-laced energy. The guys were pumped, like a college football team the week before meeting their longtime arch-rival, or a prizefighter about to get his shot at the champ. The months of training and planning were through, the date was set, and the media hype had built to a crescendo.

The following morning, we went over final details, itineraries, supply lists and cleared up any last minute questions. The last thing I did before watching the rest of the team head off to our launch base in Victoria Falls was pass out standardized forms. The heading read, "Last Will and Testament".

Angola

During the planning phase of the expedition, I'd met with all of the relevant authorities in the countries we'd be traveling through, ensuring that we had everything we needed for rite of passage through their territories. Once I secured their approval, I got insurance coverage from Lloyds of London, the only place I could find that would even consider insuring us. I also struck a deal with a specialist air extraction company who, if we got into a bind, would do what they could to get us out of there in a rush. They would also do medevacs or come and retrieve bodies as needed. Visas had been sorted out for every country except Angola. The consul there assured me that once we had the full team in country, I could submit our applications which would be processed within a few days.

We were ready to set off; not only were the visas not forthcoming, but even though I spent all day, every day, waiting in the Angolan Embassy, the people I needed to speak with fobbed me off with "Come back tomorrow and we'll take care of it."

Dave Williams and I pulled out all of the stops, leveraging every relationship we had to try and get someone with influence to help us. In the end, it was a member of Make-A-Difference's board, Bishop Moses Anderson, who in conversation with a friend of his in the U.S. Senate managed to open the door a crack and I was granted a visa to fly into Angola alone to try to sort things out.

Landing in Luanda was more than a little disconcerting. The international airport didn't even try to hide that it was in the middle of a war-torn landscape, littered with burned out vehicles.

Self preservation kicked in and I very quickly connected with a group of particularly gnarly looking South African Security Specialists who were flying in for another tour – a particularly good idea as it turned out because if I hadn't, I have no idea how I would have gotten to my hotel. Before my trip, words like airport and hotel had lulled me into a false sense of security. As a seasoned third world traveler who wasn't altogether unfamiliar with traveling through war zones, I should have known better. That thought was quickly replaced by the realization that nothing in my experience could have prepared me for this.

The next day, I was grateful to meet with and receive a security briefing at the U.S. Embassy in Luanda. Sitting comfortably in the secured area atop the hill, one of the highest points in what was once lavishly referred to as the Monte Carlo of Africa, I found out that the area I wanted to travel through was controlled by warlords. The odds of us getting through were not good, and if things went wrong on the expedition, no one was going to be able to get in to evacuate us. The Angolans were hoping that instead of admitting that they had no control over the area, they would make things inconvenient for us and we would give up and go away.

Later that afternoon, I met socially with the lovely Amanda Smit from the South African Embassy in Luanda. Over a bottle of particularly fine wine, we discussed my predicament, and she agreed to do whatever she could to help.

The following morning, after the plane's second failed attempt to take off, I decided I was getting the heck out of there. Somewhat disorientated, in no small part thanks to the mother of all hangovers, I gingerly made my way off the plane, and walking across the runway, I went towards the group of people who were striding purposefully towards me. I didn't understand what they were saying as they blathered away in what I can only imagine was very loud Portuguese. As they sneered and thrust their AK 47's toward me, it was clear that they wanted me back on the airplane. At that point, I wasn't going to argue.

The plane did finally take off on the next attempt, and we made it to Lusaka intact, where the rest of my team along with our equipment was waiting for me.

Rejoining the Team

Clearing customs and immigration, I was delighted to finally be joining my teammates, most of whom were more than happy waiting in our rented transport, a three-metric-ton DAF, a 4-wheel drive truck. It reminded me of the army trucks I'd spent a whole lot of time in a few years back. We piled into our large, olive green vehicle and made ourselves comfortable – a bunch of scruffy lads sprawled out on our therma-rest cushions, wearing shorts and t-shirts, drinking the local Mosi beer and singing songs.

As we headed off into the unknown, the adrenaline coursed through us as we bumped along in the back of our semi-covered truck. The warm African air whistled over our heads. Nobody said it, but nobody had to – we were finally embarking on the adventure of a lifetime.

Because of my flight delays, it was too late to make it to our planned campsite, but Pete, the chap who was driving us into the source, came through with a great idea. "We could go to Mr. Pete's, the best steakhouse in Lusaka. I'm friends with Pistol Pete, the owner."

Within the hour we were feasting on red meat and guzzling down cold beer and devouring our steak dinners. Seven U.S. dollars got us a thick t-bone with deep-fried french fries with just a hint of salad before rounding off the meal with tumblers filled from Pistol Pete's stash of genuine Havana rum.

Later that night, we settled down around the campfire and I brought the lads up to speed. "The beautiful Amanda Smit is in Luanda doing what she can to help us secure visas. There is an Angolan Consulate upcountry, not too far from the source of the river where we can go to get them issued if she is successful. If not, I will take a small team through 'unofficially'.

"We will travel light by night and do whatever we need to in order to get through alive. As a small stealth team, for those of us paddling, it won't be the jolly adventure that we'd all signed up for. However, if we travel quickly, with a bit of luck, we will make it uneventfully," I said as cheerfully as I could.

Then, one of the lads asked the question everyone was thinking. "What if we run across unfriendlies?"

Without having to say anything, my look answered his question, sobering both the mood and the effects of the Mosi beer and Havana Rum.

I'd not come to this decision lightly. I'd come to join the team and to get on our way as the delays had already cost us more than I'd been prepared to pay; sadly, Andy had recently chosen to drop out of the team due to commitments he had made for the period immediately after the ZZAM Expedition. Any further delays would put some of the other lads' participation in jeopardy and that would put the very expedition and everything that it stood for at risk.

Going through Angola with permission was always going to be risky anyway and we'd discussed those risks at length. There was always a chance that we were going to run into unfriendlies. If we were caught, we had official documents printed up in Portuguese promising rewards for our safe release; that was our last line of defense and was to be used only after everything else – and I mean everything else – had failed.

In the days that followed, we drove all day. It seemed that every hour or two, a village or small town would rise up out of the bush. Some villages were two or three mud huts. Others consisted of one or two dozen single-room, one-story brick houses.

Near the villages, women walked on the side of the road with towering bundles balanced on their heads. I don't know how they do it, but African women walk for miles, seemingly effortlessly carrying these bundles of firewood, jugs of water or piles of laundry wrapped in a sheet. The loads must weigh at least thirty pounds.

When we passed a village, small children jumped up and ran frantically towards the road, waving, hollering and laughing. Grown-ups just stared blankly until we waved hello from the back of the truck. Then, they immediately waved back, their faces breaking into huge sunny smiles.

We hit the relatively large town of Kitwe. It had several five-story office buildings made of glass and brick. There were also a few gas stations and restaurants. More importantly, there was the Kitwe Polo Club.

Pete, the driver, made a U-turn into the club's dirt driveway. A ruddy-faced, stocky man of about 50 walked towards us from a picnic area next to the clubhouse, where two families were gathered over cold drinks. Climbing down from the truck, I started to explain that we were headed towards the Zambezi River for an expedition. The man cut me off.

"Come on in," he said. "We have lots of cold beer, a swimming pool and hot showers. Make yourselves at home."

"Is there a campsite nearby?"

"You can camp here," said our new-found friend.

"And how much…"

"Don't worry about it," he said. "Just make yourselves at home."

The clubhouse bar had a pool table, and all the comforts of the big city. This expedition didn't seem so rough after all.

A few days later, we arrived in the town of Mwinilunga, near the source. We picked up supplies and hit the road again. We drove for about an hour on a bumpy dirt road, before pulling off on to a two-track road that seemed to materialize from nowhere in the bush. Two hundred meters down the two-track was a stand of pine trees, the kind with all their foliage up at the top, which is perfect for camping under.

We broke into the rations of rice and stew for dinner, artfully prepared by Max and Red. The stew was a soy-based imitation meat, which is not quite the same as the real thing, but it tasted pretty good. It was full of tomatoes, onions, garlic, chili peppers and assorted seasonings.

After dinner, tea was accompanied by a bottle of Bell's whiskey. It tasted great when drank from a plastic mug next to a roaring African campfire. After learning from Amanda that we weren't going to be getting our Angolan visas any time soon, I decided it was time to move on to Plan B and that a small team of us would be skulking through Angola. We had some tough conversations on this subject over the next few days, and the lads had to make their decisions.

I already had the utmost respect for each of them, and that respect grew daily. I know that for some of them, choosing to skip Angola was one of the toughest choices they would ever have to make.

At about noon the next day, we arrived at the Fisher family farm and met Pete Fisher who ran the farm. The Fisher's settled there as missionaries near the source of the Zambezi about 100 years ago. The estate, nowadays Hillwood Farm, was huge – it must have been thousands of hectares (tens of thousands of acres). After a cup of tea and introductions, Pete took us to meet his dad. We drove past the school, the butchery, the dairy, the general store, the clinic and the church, all on the same farm.

We found our way to Paul Fisher. The senior Fisher was tall, tanned and fit. Looking to be in his 60's, he wore brown shorts, knee-high socks beneath ankle-length work boots and a black felt hat with a brown leather band above its wide rim. He knew we were coming, and showed us on a map the best route to the source which was about ten miles away.

I asked him about Angola. "It's pretty dodgy right now," he said. "Nobody's in control. My advice is, if any of you have relatives who want to see you again, don't go into Angola right now."

The Source

Beneath the hand-painted sign that pointed the way to the source of the Zambezi, we stopped for the obligatory photo. Pete then maneuvered the DAF along the corrugated path until muddy ground and deep roots forced him to a halt. Ten of us, including Rory, set out on foot and quickly covered the few remaining miles.

Just as Paul Fisher had shown us on the map, the path we were on opened into a small clearing. In the center of the clearing stood a seven-foot high monument made of basketball-sized stones and just like he'd described it, there was a square of discoloration on the monument where a plaque had been anchored until thieves stole it a few years ago.

At the edge of the clearing to the left was a wooded area thick with leafy trees. A narrow path entered the woods and dropped sharply downhill into a deep ravine.

We sidestepped down the steep dirt path. It was eerie. The tree canopy above us nearly blotted out the sun. Only slivers of light twinkled through the foliage like stars in the night sky. We continued edging down the slope, made more difficult because of the carpet of fallen leaves. It was as if we were in an Indiana Jones adventure movie and were tiptoeing towards the altar inside an ancient temple.

The dank darkness was more than a little unnerving. I wasn't the only one feeling this way. None of the guys uttered a word. For the first time, there were no wisecracks, jokes or irreverence. As each man reached the bottom of the ravine, he stopped and stared at the sandy ground. All ten of us stood in a circle surrounding a gurgling stream of water. It was the source of the Zambezi River.

The inch-wide ribbon of water gurgled out of the ground, barely trickling over the sand. A few yards further down, after coursing around trees and over rocks, the ribbon widened to about two inches and rose to a depth of about a half an inch. From a mustard seed, a mighty river was born.

After a few solemn moments, we reverently walked around the area. Barry placed a foot on either side of the stream.

"Max, get a picture of me straddling the Zambezi," he whispered.

Max knelt down by the tiny pool that formed just a few yards from the source. He pulled his Nyami-Nyami necklace off over his head and dipped it in the sacred water.

I scooped a plastic film canister into the infant Zambezi water, and then meticulously taped it shut.

"Ah, she's beautiful isn't she?" Dean said to no one in particular.

Dave H., Red, Dave C. and Batch drank from the river with cupped hands. After scores of photos, the lads gathered around and I read aloud two passages from the Bible, Psalms 91 and 121. Given that we were about to put ourselves in harm's way, this passage from Psalm 91, in particular, seemed very appropriate.

If you say, "The Lord is my refuge,"
   and you make the Most High your dwelling,
   no harm will overtake you,
   no disaster will come near your tent.
For he will command his angels concerning you
   to guard you in all your ways;
   they will lift you up in their hands,
   so that you will not strike your foot against a stone.
You will tread on the lion and the cobra;
   you will trample the great lion and the serpent."

I'd sought comfort and confidence in Psalm 121 on many other occasions throughout my life, so it was only natural that I'd turn to it now. I read out loud starting at the beginning, *"I will lift up mine eyes unto the hills, from whence cometh my help. My help cometh from the Lord, which made heaven and earth,"* through the end, *"The Lord shall preserve thy going out and thy coming in from this time forth, and even for evermore."*

We all spent a while alone, each lost in his own thoughts, experiencing this magical moment. I overheard Chris asking Barry, "Why is this so important to you guys? What are you thinking now that you've seen, touched and drank from the source of the Zambezi River?"

Barry's wordless response told Chris all he needed to know.

The Beginning – No Angola

That initial blush of enthusiasm and wonder quickly dissipated as we spent the first few days of our pilgrimage dragging, kicking and cussing our sixteen foot long, one hundred pound, fire engine red expedition kayaks through the seemingly impenetrable jungle. It was hard, leaving us sunburnt, insect bitten and our skin rubbed raw by the straps that kept us leashed to our boats like pack mules.

Rocks, grass, tree limbs and thorns just laughed at our protective clothing as they slashed, gashed and bruised our flesh at will. But as we took each step and slogged our way through each mile, the tottering infant stream grew into a passable body of water and our opportunities to paddle our brand new expedition kayaks soon outgrew the necessity to drag them. The humorously irreverent banter and testosterone-laced enthusiasm had been replaced with the somber realization of why no one had ever paddled this mighty river from her source through to where she flowed into the sea. We were kicking and cussing kayaks and dealing with the inevitable and expected frustrations that bubbled to the surface as eight incredibly competent and fiercely independent bushmen plus Chris, took on an expedition together.

Front and center on all of our minds was Angola and whether or not we should go. After dinner each night, as we sat around the campfire, that was the topic that dominated our conversations. I was wearing two hats – I had put this team together to accomplish a very specific mission for a very specific purpose. A lot of time, money and energy had been invested by a lot of people to put us in a position to accomplish our goal. I saw successful completion of our River Expedition mission as a critical element in our overarching goal, which was to generate the publicity to effectively launch our Foundation so that we could make-a-difference in the lives of African amputees and many others.

When each team member had signed up and committed to come along, he had known the risks. For my river expedition teammates though, the game had changed. For all of them, paddling through Angola had been an acceptable risk providing it was officially sanctioned and legal. For some of them, the new plan I'd proposed made the risk unacceptable. I appreciated that and created the space for each guy to make his own choice. We chatted collectively and I spoke to each of them at length individually; we ended up with two teams. I was blown away by the courage and the conviction of those who chose to come with me and equally by those who made the tough choice not to.

The plan was simple. When we got to the point where the Zambezi River flowed into Angola, we'd wait for dark and I'd take Team 1 through while Team 2 drove around to meet us at Chavuma Mission, one-hundred and eighty miles downstream where the river exited Angola. If we weren't there in six days time, Team 2 would raise the alarm and initiate a recovery mission.

Ultimately, the decision was taken out of my hand. A Zambian Government Official figured out what we were up to and in a very reasonable manner, he explained that given the unacceptably high chance that we wouldn't make it through the area, we were not going to be allowed to kayak from Zambia into Angola. It would not make them look good if they let us through and we were never seen alive again. At that point, I reluctantly conceded.

When I let them know, the team's mood was all over the place; we shared a blend of extreme disappointment and profound relief. Even those of us who'd decided to give Angola a go freely admitted that it was a pretty scary prospect and the official decision, though extremely unwelcomed, had gotten us off of the hook. The extreme disappointment came from knowing that in just a few days on expedition, after all the planning, dreaming, effort and sacrifices we all made to get to this point, we'd already failed our declared mission.

"Now what?" was the question on everyone's mind. Given everything he'd done to get us to this point, I felt terrible calling Dave Williams on the satellite phone to bring him up to speed. He shared our disappointment. There was no denying our world had changed and we needed to come up with a new mission. It sucked, but it was reality.

To sit there whining and moaning didn't seem like a productive option. I apologized to Dave for my part in the breakdown and then together, we figured out what to do next. Dave and I needed to come up with a plan that took care of our primary concern – to successfully launch Make-A-Difference. We'd always seen the river trip as a means to generate publicity and achieve our goal. We saw that reconstituting the river mission from "First Full Descent of the Zambezi River led by Hippo Guy" to "Fullest Descent to date of the Zambezi River led by Hippo Guy" with the Angola drama thrown in, probably wouldn't lose us that much ground, so we decided to go with it.

Now I had to worry about my team. We all sat down with a cup of tea and I told them about the new mission. We had a pretty frank conversation where I listened to what everyone had to say as they talked about their fears, frustrations, hopes and aspirations. We spoke about everything it had taken to get us to this point and everything that we as individuals, as a team and as an organization could still accomplish. We came up with a strategy as to how we could go about doing that. Ultimately we all committed to a new plan that we were confident would take care of all concerns. Then, we threw away the tea, cracked open a bottle of whiskey and got on with it.

Instead of paddling through Angola, we loaded all our equipment back onto our truck and drove from one Zambian border post to the next. Pulling up at Chavuma Mission, we could see how the tentative waters we'd left in Zambia had grown through her adolescence in Angola and emerged as a fully-fledged, swiftly flowing river. We were all pretty excited about finally getting on the water and getting underway. Even Dave C., who'd come down with malaria, seemed to be energized by the prospect of getting on with it.

Barry and Dave unrigged their clever boat-suspension system, unloaded the kayaks and handed out the kits. Rory and Red unfolded the deflated rubber supply raft to discover a dead rat that, by the amount of damage he'd done, must have had one hell of an appetite. Our supply raft was out of commission. Everything we'd planned on filling it with now needed to fit in or on the kayaks, or be jettisoned. Everybody sorted through their kit removing anything that wasn't absolutely essential. Max gave some of our food to the villagers. "We won't eat less," he explained, "there will just be less variety."

By mid-afternoon, we overloaded our boats and it was time to say "Cheers" to Pete, Rosie and Rory. As I drifted along in my kayak watching our truck disappear in a trail of dust, I found myself extremely excited as we severed our umbilical cord to the world. It was now just us, the Zambezi River and no turning back.

We camped just above Chavuma Falls, which was more a steep rapid than a waterfall. Still, the Zambezi put on a powerful display pumping huge volumes of white water through a 50-meter wide gateway into the rock wall that stretched across the river.

"Get up Chris … you've got to see this sunrise."

It was gorgeous. Fog rose off the river, the tree line was silhouetted against the brightening sky while the white frothy rapids roared like a Boeing 747 jumbo jet howling down the runway for takeoff. Forty-five minutes after the first violet rays illuminated the horizon, the reddish-orange sun rose slowly into another azure sky as I sat sipping on yet another cup of hot tea.

Before setting off, we all stood on a rock overlooking the rapids as we agreed on the plan we made the night before. If we got the line right, the rapid would be runnable. Dean and I tested it and made it through intact and alive. Once we got to a place where we could act as a safety boat for the rest of the kayaks coming through, I noticed a whole lot of commotion up on the rocks above the rapid we'd just run.

One-by-one, the rest of the boats came through. They weren't all quite as lucky or their paddlers as skillful, as Dean pointed out. Once we'd reassembled, I asked what all the commotion had been about.

It turns out that Chris was standing on a rock wall overlooking the river taking photos when he noticed a piece of equipment that must have come loose in the river. As he reached down to grab it, he slipped off the rock into the water. Once in the water, he was quickly dragged into the middle of an aggressive rapid. He should have died and if it wasn't for Max and Barry rescuing him, he probably would have. When he made it to the shore, we left him for a while and then seeing that he was going to be okay, mercilessly made fun of him.

We were all both concerned and amused. We watched him carefully. How he responded to his swim was pretty important to the rest of us. He'd made a rookie mistake and had almost died as a result of it. In doing so, he had put the lives of two of his teammates at risk. He needed to demonstrate that he was open to learning, and then, he needed to learn and learn quickly. If he did, his teammates would do whatever they could to help him. If he didn't, I'd have to send him home at our next re-supply point. I wasn't prepared to carry the risk.

I was grateful that he stuck with us for several reasons – I liked the guy, I needed a journalist and it would have been a nightmare and a huge pain in the arse to get him out of there.

Chris provided a lot of humor for the rest of us during the next few days as he developed a very close bond with his life jacket. He did everything that was asked of him and then some and he didn't complain. Most importantly, if he didn't know something, he asked for help and then accepted it. It didn't take him long to become a universally respected and accepted teammate and a huge asset to our team.

Pretty soon, we got into the day-by-day of expedition work. The river changed. Now, she was a couple hundred yards wide with little current and rolling hills on either side. The wildlife had all been shot by the locals and presumably eaten, and after days of paddling, the scenery was pretty uninspiring. Our bodies adapted. We got stronger and we needed to, as our preparation hadn't trained us for how taxing this expedition had become. As the days turned into weeks, routines and roles emerged. From time to time we all annoyed each other, but for the most part, we got along.

Every morning, Dave H. would get up at 5:00 a.m., start a fire, and put the kettle on for tea. At 6:00 a.m. he called reveille. If that didn't work, he would blast us with a verbal barrage of abuse until everyone got out of their tents. Dave C. sometimes assisted Dave H. with the morning wake-up call. The two amigos often launched into a morning radio dee-jay skit, loosely modeled on the Robin Williams character in the movie *Good Morning Vietnam*.

Dave C. would start, "Rise and shine campers. It's 6:05 in the a.m. The temperature is barely above freezing on the banks of the Zambezi, but the sun is coming up. The forecast is for scorching heat and plenty of painful paddling."

Then Dave H. chimed in, "And now campers, it's time for riverside aerobics. Touch your left index finger to your right elbow, and hold. 1, 2, 3 … feel the burn … 4, 5 … and release."

Some mornings, the duo would break into song. My favorite mornings were the ones when we were serenaded by the song "I Believe in Miracles" from the movie *The Full Monty*. It was one of their favorites. As I said earlier, Dave H. has a pleasing, melodic singing voice. Unfortunately, Dave C. does not.

We quickly became the high performing team I knew we could be, each fulfilling his requisite, clearly defined roles. Dave H. had firmly established himself in the role of Drill Sergeant.

"Time check," he would say. "7:05, twenty-five minutes till we're on the river."

We got an update every five minutes. Dave H. was always the first one into his boat. On the river, he paddled at a maniacal rate of eighty strokes a minute. The rest of us averaged between fifty and sixty.

"I figure after one month, I'll have done 1,066,340 strokes," he announced from his tent one night. Eight sets of eyes rolled heavenward in unison.

The more difficult the task, the more Dave H. seemed to enjoy it. "Make it harder," was his motto. On the river, he was the team's conscience. If we said we were stopping for lunch at 11:30, Dave H. made sure we didn't stop until 11:30, even if we passed an island of paradise at 11:25. The rest of us regularly cussed him, but that just added to his enjoyment.

Our weekly menu wouldn't make any cookbooks. It barely provided enough nourishment to replace the thousands of calories we burned daily. For breakfast every day, we ate a bowl of cereal with a cup of tea. The cereal was dry parchment-like flakes that formed a gray paste much like baby cereal when mixed with water. "One serving contained the nutritional equivalent of two eggs, a slice of toast and two rashers of bacon," chimed Batch, eagerly eating two bowls each morning. The rest of us were lucky to choke down one.

Red, who was always the last to emerge from his sleeping bag, hastily stuffed a couple handfuls of this dry cereal into his mouth before jumping into his boat. That's like eating two handfuls of sawdust, but with less flavor.

Midway through the morning and afternoon paddle, we would usually stop for one handful of GORP (Good Ole Raisins and Peanuts) and another cup of tea. Lunch was usually a portion of the previous night's dinner, some candy and another cup of tea.

By 3:30, we'd usually begin our search for a campsite. At first, good camping spots were plentiful. There'd be lots of dry level ground with accessible banks, and long stretches of nice sandy beach.

Once in camp, everyone quickly jockeyed for the best real estate; then, tents were pitched while a rotating crew of three or four adventurers set off in search of firewood. There were days when dry, hard firewood was plentiful and there were days when it was not.

Max started dinner by 5:00 and served it by 6:00. Dinner six days a week was stew made from rice, soya-based imitation meat and dehydrated vegetables. Once a week we had stew from pasta, soya-based imitation meat, dehydrated vegetables and more tea. Though the ingredients at his disposal were limited, Max became a master with a 20-liter pot warmed by a wood fire. He enjoyed his reputation as an excellent cook.

After tea around the campfire, everyone crawled into their tents by 7:30 p.m. depending on the level of attack mounted by the mosquitoes. It would be dark by then in the Southern Hemisphere's winter.

Like a typical winter in Africa, with its upsides and downsides, even though the mosquitoes were out in force, the wide varieties of other bugs had not yet started swarming. The days were actually quite comfortable once the sun was up and arching across the almost always cloudless sky. The temperature hovered around the low-to-mid-80s Fahrenheit. Any trace of humidity was fanned away by a brisk headwind that blew over us all day long. The sun only switched to blast furnace mode from about 2:30 till 3:30 in the afternoon, but it was bearable. It was nothing like the African summer heat.

The nights were something else entirely. I'd estimate the mercury plunged to the low 40's Farenheit. We were grateful for the fleece jackets with our kit. Each night got colder and we would don more layers of clothing.

We knew that as the expedition progressed, it would only get colder. Winter peaked in Africa in early to mid-July, exactly when we planned to be in the gorge below Victoria Falls. There, the sun wouldn't peek past the gorge's deep sheer walls till late morning. It disappeared by early afternoon, and the air didn't warm much.

For the time being, the trick was to get up, fold the tents and pack as energetically as possible. Then, we would plant our posteriors near the blazing fire and sip hot tea until the sun climbed over the horizon at around 6:45 a.m. The next part of the morning drill was to strip off all our warm clothes except shorts and t-shirts and leap into the boats. Five minutes of vigorous paddling later, our teeth stopped chattering.

The paddling was endless. It was tough work that got tougher as the day wore on. At fifty to sixty strokes a minute for most of us, the quiet "slap, splash, slap, splash" of the double-blade paddles dipping rhythmically in and out of the water induced a Zen-like trance if not for the searing pain that gripped our backs, shoulders and neck muscles.

The first few days had been tough, but after a week, our muscles and joints adapted. The pain dulled to an ache. The team had pulled muscles and pinched nerves, but nothing made them complain. Early on,

I'd discovered a design fault with my paddle. With extended stretches of paddling, it rubbed away an inch of flesh just below my elbow. Barry and Dave H., the team medics, kept a close eye on the wound to ensure that it didn't become infected and we eventually came up with a pretty novel way of strapping my arm so that it could heal while I continued paddling. Not wanting to be a liability, I hadn't mentioned my injury to Barry and Dave H. right away, and when they initially strapped it up, I told everyone it was fine.

At first I lied. Then, the pain had actually gone away. When we changed the dressing a few hours later, my arm was a bloody mess. The brace had chewed greedily through more flesh to bone. All these years later, I still bear the scars of that particular bout with stupidity. Instead of taking it easy for the afternoon and asking for help when I needed it, I'd tried to macho it out which had only made it a lot more difficult for me and my team. I was and am disabled and I needed to accept it quickly because my ego was writing checks that my teammates had to cover. They were okay with my disability and picking up the slack that my limitations presented. It was my stupidity that annoyed, disappointed and worried them. My team didn't need me to be a superstar paddler; they needed me to be a superstar leader.

That said, we all had our own challenges. Something we could all agree on was that fatigue built throughout the day made the last two hours of paddling an exercise in physical and psychological endurance.

After a few weeks on the river, the lads became tetchy due to the monotony of the river. But her complexion soon changed into the Barotse Floodplain, bloating to over twenty miles wide. For over a week, we saw very little terra firma as we tried to navigate the maze of channels; more often than not, luck trumped skill as we made our way through. Once the sun set, the air became so thick with bugs, we had to chew to breathe. Unsurprisingly we saw very few people. Most of them were headed towards the mainland as the water levels rose and the floodplain flooded. We truely lucked out in that we got to witness the immemorial Ku-om-boka ceremony that marked the Lozi King, the Litunga, moving from one palace to another on higher ground. The polers on his giant royal dugout barge were spectacular specimens of men whose Cirque du Soleil strength and coordination were nothing short of amazing.

After a beer laden, fun-filled celebration, our adventure continued. The river morphed once again after the Barotse, her adolescence apparent as she rushed and paused between and around the islands. Wildlife was reappearing, and one night, we learned of a five-meter croc who'd climbed ashore at night and snatched a 30-year-old man who was sleeping outside his hut in a nearby village. It's unusual for crocs to go ashore for their food. After the incident, panic swept through the village like a brush fire.

The villagers were going to launch a crocodile massacre until the local lodge manager, Ryan, pleaded with them not to. He said if they gave him a chance, he would kill the offending reptile. Plus he'd prove to the villagers it was that animal that had devoured the 30-year-old villager, saving the rest of the crocs from death.

Ryan set a simple trap; a hole in the ground covered with brush and a piece of meat suspended over it. Within 24 hours, a croc took the bait, dropping headfirst into the hole. Ryan found him the next morning. The croc was so big that he was unable to turn his body around and climb out. The croc was swiftly dispatched with a .22 caliber slug to his brain.

Ryan took the croc to the village where the man had been carried off. With all the residents gathered around him, Ryan slit the predator's belly from tail to gullet. There was the barely decomposed body of the 30-year-old man.

It was sobering stuff, and we knew that we needed to keep our wits about us as we continued on our quest. In addition to the wildlife that had gone from non-existent, to occasional to prolific, our apprehension increased. During one of our check in calls on the satellite phone we'd learned that one of the internationals, an expert kayaker who'd been drawn to the huge whitewater of the mighty Zambezi, had drowned. A whirlpool had swallowed him and held him underwater for more than four minutes before releasing his lifeless body. We had a week of huge whitewater before us.

Six weeks and, on average, twelve pounds lighter, we arrived at Victoria Falls, the psychological halfway point of the expedition. It was a mixed blessing. We got a chance to rest as we prepared for the Batoka Gorge. The next week would have us paddling through some of the largest whitewater in the world. Batch and a few of our whitewater specialists went up in a helicopter to take a look. The footage Batch brought back was not at all promising. The rapids were huge with waterfalls and slides complicating some of the runs. We saw that the eddies were small and the margin for error virtually non-existent as we sat through the video the first time. The team all gathered around. Few words were spoken except the occasional groan or "No way!!" punctuating the silence.

The team went to work carefully dissecting each and every stretch of the river, each rapid and each safety eddy. A few hours later we had a plan; there was a way to run this stretch of river and we could do it. Sitting in that room, it was an absolute pleasure to watch the team at work. Numerous opinions were offered by a group of eminently qualified and experienced river guides, and it all culminated in one team decision. Only time would tell if our plan would work, and God willing, we'd all survive to tell the tale.

Before we got to enjoy the whitewater, I still had some unfinished business to take care of. We still had to paddle past the exact spot where I'd had my body and my life ripped apart; it was the spot where Evans had died and where the frenzied event had changed a lot of lives. I was more than a little nervous as we made our way down the river. Our boats glided silently through the water. No one said much. Just ahead of us, the mist rose up to the heavens above Victoria Falls. The roaring water crashed onto the rocks hundreds of feet from where it began along the mile long lip of the rock wall. It all served as the backdrop to my tale to the lads as we drifted by the spot.

I was eerily calm as I pointed to where the hippo must have been hiding. As I recounted my experience, I pointed out the different landmarks. I pointed out the spot where I'd been ripped apart, where I'd swam, where Mike had rescued me, the rocks I'd been patched up on and where Evans had died. We stopped. I said a prayer. We all took a moment to reflect. Then suddenly, a giant bull hippo lunged out of the water from the exact spot we thought my hippo must have been hiding. His jaws were wide open as he seemingly zeroed in on me for a direct hit before crashing into the water a couple of feet away. Everything was happening in slow motion. I was sharing a kayak with Red. He said he could hear me repeating, "Not again. Not again. I can't do it again." And then, just as quickly as the hippo appeared, it disappeared, and we never saw it again. Now, I could get on with surviving the Batoka Gorge.

When it came to the next stretch of the river, we all accepted that if someone swam, they would in all likelihood die and we probably wouldn't be able to retrieve their body until the water levels dropped in a couple of months time. Even as a veteran river guide, I was terrified at the prospect of going through the gorge, so I put Max in charge of getting us safely through the next stretch as he was more competent than I was when it came to getting people safely through huge whitewater. Once again, our team worked together like the consummate professionals we were. Max did an awesome job getting us all through alive. He sought input when appropriate and was decisive when he needed to be. He was confident which made the rest of us confident. We were all used to being in charge, but for the sake of the success and the survival of our team, we deferred to Max's leadership.

The next month was hell. We needed to paddle across two huge lakes. Lake Kariba, volume-wise, is the largest man-made lake in the world at 140 miles long and up to 20 miles wide. When we finally traversed it, we thought that the six-foot swells and wind blowing in our face was probably the toughest thing that any of us would ever deal with. A week later, we got to Lake Cahora Bassa, the fourth largest lake in Africa at 180 miles long and up to 24 miles wide. It made crossing Lake Kariba seem like a lazy beach holiday.

There was more wind and bigger swells, so much so that one day we didn't even try to get into the water. We were even forced to paddle by moonlight one night, which at first blush doesn't sound that worrisome until you consider that we were heading across wide-open water, navigating by nothing more than sight, sound and intuition. We were dodging hippos by their sputtering warning calls and splashes as they dove for safety. Whether we were camping or paddling, we couldn't afford for one moment to forget that we were sharing the lake with some of the largest and most aggressive crocodiles known to man. They were angry in part because they were hungry, thanks to man's encroachment.

We were all ridiculously relieved to have Lake Cahora Bassa behind us. We were also exhausted - physically, mentally, and emotionally. Paddling across Lake Cahora Bassa had been a horrible experience for all of us. I couldn't have been more proud of my team and the way we'd hung in there and worked together. Now as a team, we had some tough choices to make. Sitting around the campfire, I laid it out for the lads. Red had figured out exactly how far we had to go to the Indian Ocean which was the finish line. We all knew that some of the guys had to be back to work in two weeks time. This gave us twelve days to reach the ocean to allow two days more for those with work contracts to get home.

"344 miles to the finish in a straight line," Red said. "If we're going to make it to the end before those with contracts have to leave us, we need to cover about 31 miles a day in a straight line."

Straight-line distance doesn't account for the twists and turns the river takes. Covering 31 miles a day in a straight line means following the river as it winds its way to the ocean. We would actually have to paddle closer to 40 or 50 miles a day. That meant 10 hours a day in the water. The maps didn't have much detail, so we had no idea whether we could make that grueling schedule.

We had to make two crucial decisions. We needed to decide, as a team, if we were willing to bust our butts and push hard through the final leg of the trip to accommodate our teammates with work contracts. If the team decided to go for it, those with contracts needed to decide if they wanted to risk losing their jobs if we didn't make it to the ocean on time. The hard fact was, once our re-supply team left, the only way home for those who stuck around, was on the river.

Someone asked Red if he thought it was possible for us to cover that much distance in that short a time.

"It's possible," he said, with his map spread out in front of him. "If weather conditions are good, if the river doesn't wander too much and if everybody's body holds up, we can do it. We are going to have to bust our arses to do this. And if we do make it, we'll be really broken at the end."

Mozambique is a beautiful country. Because of the years of nasty civil war, there are few people who have seen the Zambezi where it flows through that rugged country. After two and a half months on the river, it seemed a shame to rush through the final two weeks and diminish what should have been a special moment, the final chapter of an amazing life experience.

Among those with no work commitments, the vote was unanimous. We'd do everything we could to finish our mission in the next 12 days. Among those with work commitments, the vote was the same. I never really thought for a moment that it would be any other way.

The next morning the local priest, Father Claude, and 32 children from his parish spent four and a half hours helping us portage our kayaks and equipment. They guided us along a very vague mountainside path through a minefield, so that we could restart our expedition just below the dam wall. Three of the guys, Dean, Chris and Red inadvertently missed a turn and had to backtrack out of an "unsafe zone." Max, our resident landmine clearing expert wasn't amused and made it abundantly clear to all of us that we really needed to get our act together as we were slap bang in the middle of what was one of the most heavily land-mined areas in the world.

According to Father Claude, there were four rapids in the Cabora Bassa Gorge, "and none of them should pose much of a problem."

Three hours after setting off, we'd already run six rapids. The rapids weren't big, but they were vicious. Everybody ran the first three rapids without incident, but the fourth was a different story.

As Dave H. and I dropped into the fourth rapid, we got sideswiped by a powerful wave and capsized almost immediately. We tried half a dozen times to roll upright but failed. We signaled each other to eject and Dave H. did what he was supposed to do. I couldn't. I was trapped in my cockpit. After being thrashed about as I struggled to release the paddle that was attached to my arm, I managed to cut loose, but then, as I tried to eject from my kayak, my feet got caught on a dry bag wedged between my legs and left me dangling upside down. The current was so strong that I couldn't bend forward to dislodge my legs. Spotting that all was not well, Dave H. took a deep breath, let go of the kayak and then swam underwater, to free my legs. I popped to the surface, gasping for air only to see Dave H., sucked into a huge whirlpool as he began a deep and nasty swim.

Dave H. fought below the surface for about 20 seconds before he resurfaced and started to swim towards a pool of calm water between two rock outcroppings on the right bank. As he put his head down and started stroking, we spotted a 14-foot croc slip into the water from the base of the rocks. He was stalking Dave who was less than 30 feet away and swimming right at him.

We all started yelling at Dave H., but Batch, who was fortunately nearby, frantically stroked his kayak between Dave H. and the croc, landed a well placed blow on the croc's snout with his paddle while screaming, "Climb on! Croc!" Dave H. didn't need to be told twice as he scrambled atop the kayak's bow. The croc disappeared underwater. He would have to find lunch someplace else today.

We all paddled to shore and started the now well-rehearsed process of draining the boat, sorting the gear and chalking up another swim for the capsized kayakers. Since the ZZAM Expedition began, we kept a running tally of how many times each person had to swim. It was our "Hall of Shame." The tally adds a little levity to dire situations that could have killed any of us.

The tiny beach we stood on was barely big enough for the eight of us. Dave H. started to walk into the weeds at the base of the mountain, but Max stopped him.

"That could be a minefield," Max said.

Dave H. did an immediate about-face and returned to the group. "I capsized in a rapid, got sucked 20 feet under by a whirlpool, just missed being eaten by a croc, and then, when I finally got to shore, was surrounded by landmines. It was just another fun-filled afternoon on the ZZAM Expedition."

Mozambique was turning into a land of extremes. Extreme beauty, hardship, danger and kindness of the people we ran into.

We made it through the gorge without losing anyone and then a couple of days later we passed what seemed to be a public beach. There were about 100 people wading in knee-deep water, adults washing themselves and children laughing and splashing. We paddled along the edge of a giant sand bar 200 yards from the riverbank, far from the public bathers.

Fifty yards ahead, there was something in the water that we mistook for a hippo. As we approached, the figure didn't move. It was not an animal. We drew closer and discovered that it was the floating corpse of a teenage African boy.

He was lying face down in a foot of water, his knees tucked under him and arms dangling lazily at his sides. His face was buried in the sand. His bluish-purple skin started to bloat. It didn't seem like anyone on the beach even noticed him.

Red pulled out the Global Positioning Satellite receiver and jotted down the coordinates so we could tell the police where to find the body. We discussed our options.

"If we go to the police and tell them about this floater, we are then responsible for it," Max said. "Most likely, they'll detain us for two or three days while they retrieve the body, take reports and conduct interviews. And if nobody claims the body, we'll have to arrange and pay for the funeral and burial. That's how it works in Mozambique."

If we were to get held up for two days, we wouldn't reach the Indian Ocean on time. Whilst we discussed what to do, two men paddled up in a dug-out canoe. We told them about the corpse. Max talked to them in Portuguese. They weren't quite sure how to react to what Max said and we all suspected that his imperfect Portuguese was losing something in the translation. The paddlers appeared both indifferent and at the same time agreeable. It seemed the dead kid was common knowledge. We paddled off in silence.

Somehow or other, we covered the distance we needed to each day. Though morale was good and determination intact, we were all physically breaking down. At about 4:00 a.m. one morning, we were woken by the sound of Red vomiting outside his tent. He was suffering from dehydration and exhaustion. Out of all of us, Red was the most motivated to finish on time; his daughter Taryn was about to be born. He was also hurting the most.

In close second was Max. While paddling that afternoon, Max leaned over the side of the kayak, vomited, and barely missing a stroke, went right back to paddling. My arm had been numb for several days and the numbness was spreading to my neck and the side of my head. On average we'd all lost more than 25 pounds and we had long since burned all our fat and were now burning muscle. This was not a holiday. It was an expedition. But by the same token, my primary commitment and responsibility was to make sure that everyone got home alive.

As we set up camp one night, we were a week or so from the end. I made the rounds, checking in with each of the lads. I listened to what they had to say and what they held back, but their bodies revealed. I listened to their hopes and their concerns. I was torn over what to do. I considered making an "executive decision" to back off the murderous pace. I felt like apologizing to those who'd lose their jobs, to Red who would miss the birth of his daughter, to Carrie, who'd taken two weeks off work to travel half way around the world to meet me at the end of the expedition and to the folks from the BBC and *Carte Blanche* who were en route to capture the historic finish. I listened, thought and prayed. We continued.

We met up with Carrie, the folks from the BBC, Rory, our re-supply team and a film crew at the village of Caia, where a pretty disheveled and somewhat overwhelmed Carrie was waiting, wondering what she'd been thinking when she decided to travel to one of the most remote, dangerous spots on the planet to see me. In her research, she knew that along the brief stretch of river, there were landmines, bandits, crocodiles, hippopotamus, Zambezi sharks and even more danger. All the same, there she stood alone, to the side, waiting for me to arrive.

With two days left to cover sixty-two straight-line miles of river, we still had quite a job on our hands. Carrie and the rest of the folk's arrival had provided fresh food and a welcomed, albeit brief distraction, but we still had a lot of ground to cover.

Rory, Carrie and Derek Watts, a well-known television news journalist, joined us, following unobtrusively in a dingy with a motor on it. We were well and truly on the final stretch and most of us felt reenergized except for Red. Red now had malaria and was going downhill fast. The closest spot for a medevac was the airstrip at the little village of Chinde, our final destination. I was relieved to have Carrie along. As a registered nurse, she was able to keep an eye on Red and support Dave H., our medic. That said, the gods were smiling on us. We were blessed with very little wind. Even the few drops of water falling from the sky couldn't dampen our excitement. Just then, a somersaulting hippo with its jaws agape got a little too close to Dave C. and Dean, reminding us that the expedition was not over.

The next morning, we woke up to a steel gray overcast sky that threatened to storm. We ate quickly and though there were grins on everyone's drawn bearded faces, there was little conversation.

As we drank tea, took down tents and packed the boats, it dawned on me – this was the last time we'd do this. This shouldn't have come as a surprise, but it did. This routine had lasted three months. It became our life. It was natural, even comfortable, and we were accustomed to it. Now, it was about to end.

A thick fog hovered above the river. After we'd been on the water an hour, the rain began. It continued on and off throughout the day. We paddled on mechanically in a daze of exhaustion. It was not how we thought the expedition would end when we stood solemnly at the source three months ago.

At 1:00 p.m., we didn't stop for lunch; Red assured us we were only six miles from the Indian Ocean. We pushed on, again with little conversation. We weren't giddy with excitement. Everyone seemed flat.

We paddled on through the cold rain, and came to a right bend in the river. The river narrowed now; it was about 100 yards wide and lined on both sides by tall trees. We kept our boats in a tight formation within a few yards of each other, but no one spoke.

We rounded the bend and there, about a mile away, was our goal – the end of the ZZAM expedition. Nobody said a word, but we all stopped paddling. We just sat there with our paddles laid across our cockpits and stared at the sea.

Through the cold, misty air, we could see the waves breaking where the Zambezi flared out and merged into the Ocean.

I was emotionally flat. Looking at the other seven guys, I could see that they were too. It may have been the exhaustion, or the settling realization that it was over. It was too much to process all at once.

After a few minutes I lifted my paddle. "Let's go to the ocean, guys."

We started paddling, and suddenly, emotions started to well up in me. They weren't separate, distinct, identifiable emotions, but a swirling churning mix. Somebody said he was getting goose bumps. Another had a lump in his throat. For the most part, we paddled in silence.

We could see a crowd gathered on the right shore, about 200 yards ahead. We all exchanged glances and without a word, picked up the pace. We could see the finish line, the town of Chinde. It was the last stop on the Zambezi.

There was no white sand beach or a banner fluttering in the breeze saying, "Congratulations ZZAM Team." There was no reception committee. There wasn't even any sunshine. Chinde was an abandoned shipyard, a riverside graveyard littered with rusted corpses of ships that hadn't been seaworthy for decades.

We found no adoring crowds, only a group of 50 or so villagers who knew nothing of the ZZAM Expedition. They gathered to gawk at the grungy white guys in red kayaks.

For the final 60 seconds of the ZZAM Expedition, we dug in hard, our paddles whipping through the air, cutting swift and clean through the water. As we neared the bank, we put in a final, hard push, and ran our boats aground onto the wet, hard-packed gray sand of the beach with a thud. We were done. It was finished.

Slowly, we pried ourselves out of our boats and stared blankly at one another. It wasn't quite registering. The team gathered around a boat and we all shook hands. But now what?

We looked at the crowd of people staring at us, the rusting hulks rotting on shore, and the large garbage strewn village set among the trees in the distance. Now what?

Derek Watts emerged from the crowd with a video camera. He focused on us and asked how we felt. Our answers were short, and less than profound.

"You guys seem a bit overwhelmed. Perhaps it will take awhile for this to sink in." Derek said.

We were standing on shore next to our boats. Nobody moved. We didn't know what to do.

I expected revelry, joy and sunshine. I expected to plow into the ocean, turn the boats around and return triumphantly to the shore, to a white sand beach with throngs of admirers and media waiting to congratulate us and celebrate with us, amid blaring trumpets and singing angels.

The locals continued staring at us as if they expected some sort of dog-and-pony show as Batch filmed an interview I did with Derek. Two agitated AK-47 bearing policemen made their way toward us, and so did Eric, a tall, thickset white man, a British Aid Consultant.

After a few minutes, I took Eric to meet Carrie and the lads and to let them know that the cops thought we were mercenaries or spies. Leaving our boats and equipment, we took the half-mile walk through the village. We passed by dozens of thatch huts with fish drying on the roofs. Mangy dogs and brightly colored chickens scattered as we approached. Every villager stopped to stare as we walked by. We got to the house provided to

Eric by his British employers. The entire structure was whitewashed and surrounded by an elevated porch. A generator sat in the backyard.

The rest of the team went inside with Eric to drink some beer and discuss this weird final chapter. I spent the next half hour in the yard with the agitated policeman who had a half-dozen reinforcements and was yelling so hard, his face contorted and veins popped out from his forehead. Meanwhile, his AK-47 dangled ominously from a strap over his shoulder. We were placed under house arrest and unable to leave the premises until we met with the police chief in the morning.

I shrugged and said "OK," then returned inside the house. I didn't care. We had somewhere for Red to rest and being under house arrest with a refrigerator full of beer was the kind of trouble we could handle.

A little later, it was just the ZZAM Team gathered together, perhaps for the last time. It was clear from the perplexed look on the guys' faces that it hadn't quite sunk in. The ZZAM Expedition was finished. Mission accomplished. I took the opportunity to salute the team I handpicked. I was overwhelmed with pride and gratitude for being granted the privilege to lead these exceptional men.

Raising a beer, I toasted, "Gentlemen, to a job well done. Let us drink a toast – not to the finish of the ZZAM Expedition, but to the three months and 2,700 kilometers that brought us here. Cheers!"

Post ZZAM
Summer 1998

The morning after we were arrested, I went with the BBC correspondent to talk to the police chief. He apologized profusely and said we were free to come and go as we wished. We managed to get everyone where they needed to be on time. Unfortunately Red's malaria became Blackwater Fever and he ended up in the hospital for a while, but did make it to his daughter's birth.

I half-heartedly tried to show Carrie a good time as we took a brief vacation in Zimbabwe before she had to head back to work and her life.

It took me a while to get used to the idea that the expedition was done. I did a few radio interviews. I had no trouble telling stories about the adventure and the good and bad times we had. I did and still do find it difficult to articulate my feelings, to express how the Zambezi River and the ZZAM Expedition changed me.

I changed, there is no doubt. I'm not the same man who stood at the source of the Zambezi, looking down on the river as it bubbled up from subterranean depths and began its 2,700 km journey through Africa to the Indian Ocean.

It may be cliché, but the ZZAM Expedition was a spiritual journey for all of us. Nyami-Nyami, the River God, seemed to purge the baggage of civilized life that had no place on the river. Our titles were stripped away – son, brother, African, American, Englishman, uncle, businessman, father, fiancé – none were applicable on the Zambezi. Whether or not I married Carrie, whether I lived in Africa or America, the status of my retirement plan, the path of my career, none of it mattered.

As Batch said in an email after the trip:

This was a unique opportunity, to be thrown into an expedition almost totally removed from one's normal environment, where all the day-to-day stresses, strains, comforts and pleasures were absent. Our lives were totally simplified, without the BS. It was a three-month stretch where the slate was wiped clean. We were invited to forget about everything that we knew and were familiar with and leave it behind. We were given a new, simpler environment and set of parameters in which to operate. Our needs became more basic. We became a lot closer to the basic human animal than we ever could in our normal city lives.

I didn't find myself missing my car, my down comforter, my computer or my work. Rather, I missed my girlfriend, my family and my friends. People are just so much more important now.

Chapter 7

Building a New Life

Getting a Proper Job
Fall 1998

On the flight back to America, Chris and I drank a lot of beer and chatted about what might lie ahead for us both as we flew the friendly skies towards the inevitable challenge of reentering society. It would take some adjusting as we had spent the last few months absorbed in coping with the day-to-day monotony of paddling down the river and the business of surviving.

We realized that we were ill-equipped for whatever it was that lay ahead. Having spent so much time removed from civilization, we were now faced with the very real and daunting prospect of figuring out how to reenter society at large. More importantly, we needed to figure out how to pick up our relationships with those nearest and dearest to us.

Somehow "Hi, we're back! That was an awesome river trip!" wasn't going to cut it for me or for the people I cared about. The last few months had drawn us all into a level of introspection not possible in the world outside ZZAM. Who we were, how we perceived ourselves, our relationships with others, and our roles within society was no longer clear.

On the river, it had been simple. Each of us knew exactly what our roles and responsibilities were and what we needed to do to survive and successfully complete our mission. There was no room or tolerance for ego or personal agenda and for the duration of our mission, we trusted one another with our very lives.

As the leader, my role was crystal clear. I was to make sure that we all did what we said we'd do. I had to sustain confidence and ambition in my teammates so that we could take care of each other and accomplish our goals. We had taken the notion of operating as a high-performing team to the extreme. Having lived that way so intensely and for such an extended period of time made readjusting to the real world a bit tricky. On the river, ensuring that we maintained a productive mood had been far more important than pandering to each individual's feelings. Now back in the real world, I needed to move more carefully and orientate to a different set of standards.

It was fun at first. The interest in us was flattering and inflated our egos, but soon, the follow-up interviews and dinners were over and we were left to get on with life. We were ending up in bars way too often, drinking too much, wallowing in our perceived former glories and muttering the cliché, "They just don't get it." We failed at first to use our experience to spring into a bright new future. We hung on to our past glories, convinced that we'd experienced the best that life had to offer. We were miserable, and true to the cliché, misery loves company. Chris and I were spending a lot of time together reinforcing negativity in each other's lives.

I was spending my days editing the video footage that Batch had filmed. By day, I was back on the Zambezi. At night I'd go to Carrie's apartment and try to stay positive about our future. Carrie was an absolute star. She knew how to deal with me; she knew when to back off and she did that for a while. As a testament to the depths of her love, and my extreme good fortune, she agreed to become my wife when I proposed to her, never doubting that the man she'd fallen in love with would emerge from the fog.

We successfully launched Make-A-Difference and one of our first fundraisers after the ZZAM Expedition was The Marathon of Hope. It was an ultra-marathon. When Dave Williams first mentioned the idea, I had no idea what an ultra-marathon was. It turns out that it's an event where individuals and teams see how far they can run in twenty-four hours. I found the race quite tough. The event was moderately successful in the publicity it raised and the funds it generated, and extremely successful in terms of the statement it made. Make-A-Difference was here to stay.

Last Days in Zimbabwe

As our wedding day drew closer, I returned to Zimbabwe to close down the life that I'd been living there. I had to let go of the lease on my apartment and sell all my possessions to help pay for our wedding. I also had to let Edna go. When I first returned from England after my accident and subsequent treatment, I rented an apartment and set up home. Edna Kunaka, all two hundred plus pounds of her, was working as a maid and nanny for my sister, Lisa.

One day, Edna showed up at my apartment and declared that she would be looking after me, and she did for the next few years. While her skills as a maid and a cook left a lot to be desired, it was her companionship that I valued most. Matronly in manner and appearance, Edna was semi-literate, spoke very little English, and spoke even less when she was mad. She was devoutly religious and had lived a pretty tough life. Her daughter had died the year before, her son was unemployed and her husband, though he may have loved her, didn't treat her well at all; he drank too much, beat her up when he was drunk and made no secret of the fact that he loved the ladies.

Yet around me, she never failed to lift my spirits, ease my frustrations and help me keep a positive attitude and laugh at life. She showed me that life was as simple a game as I wanted it to be. It wasn't the hand a person was dealt that mattered so much as how it was played. She was one of my angels so it was with very heavy hearts that 'Gogo' as she referred to herself, and I parted ways.

There were a lot of goodbyes. Some were nodding acquaintances, others were good friends. I said goodbye to my family. I knew we would see each other in the future, but I was saying goodbye to the days, months and years that lay between now and then; the dinners, the cups of tea, the commiserations and the celebrations that I would miss. I said goodbye to my pets, the people of my homeland, the vibrant sunrises, bold sunsets, the brilliance of the Msasa trees, the smell of the first rains, the song of cicadas, drums around the fires beating through the night, the mud huts, the wildlife and the Zambezi River. I said goodbye to my way of life in Africa, but it was okay because I knew I was exchanging it for a life with Carrie in America.

Marriage
August 28, 1999

Our wedding day was one of the most joyful days of my life to date, but the rehearsal the night before was not. A lot of the people I cared about were there; my Mum and Stewart, some of my family from England and Anton and his new wife Kim had all flown into town to be with me to celebrate our nuptials. Going through the motions at St. Michaels, the Catholic church that Carrie had attended all of her life, I'd been a gibbering wreck; I was sweating like a pig and shaking like a leaf as the enormity of the situation finally hit me. By marrying Carrie I was choosing a new life in a new land and in doing so, I was walking away from almost everyone and everything I knew and loved.

However, as I stood there at the front of the church on the day, my dear friend Bishop Moses Anderson officiating, my groomsmen in their finery, the pews filled with family and friends, I couldn't have been calmer or more confident. Then I saw Carrie. As cliché as it sounds, I nearly lost my breath when I saw her gliding down the aisle more beautiful than anyone or anything I'd ever seen. I was exactly where I was supposed to be, and I was doing exactly what I was supposed to be doing.

When we got back from our honeymoon in Hawaii, it was time to get on with the reality of starting a new life. We were living in Carrie's one bedroom apartment in a complex referred to as "the ghetto." Carrie was supporting us on her salary as a nurse and given what we'd spent on our wedding, we were flat broke. There wasn't a great demand for one-armed safari guides in the Metro Detroit area, and my lack of formal training in any other relevant field, coupled with my ego, resulted in me not having an income for a while – but I wasn't overly concerned. I was busy launching a company. My best man at my wedding, Billy, and I were importing African art and furniture. Billy was already successful in his own right and he'd invested the money we needed to set up a company that we hoped would make us a lot of money and allow me to keep one foot in Africa while living in America.

As the days turned into weeks, my self-esteem plummeted and I began wondering what the hell I'd done. I felt inadequate as a husband, as a business partner, as a friend and as a member of society. I started feeling sorry for myself and backed away from life, from Carrie, from Make-A-Difference, from Billy and from everything else. My health was deteriorating. Given that one of my lungs had been violated by a hippo's tusk, I guess I really shouldn't have been surprised when from time to time I'd just stop breathing; some thought that I was drinking too much. Life sucked and I was doing a great job acting like a victim of my circumstances.

One morning the phone rang; it was my Mum. "Red is in the hospital. He had an accident and he probably isn't going to make it."

My mind went to the last time I'd been with Red. I'd been driving rather badly as we rushed to the airport, trying to get him there in time to catch his flight. We were running late because we'd been deep in conversation and had lost track of the time. He was sharing with me the experiences that made up his new life as a dad. He was telling me how much he loved his new baby daughter Taryn, how she meant the world to him, made him happier and prouder than he had ever imagined he could be, and how she gave his life purpose. He was committed to doing whatever he could for her for the rest of his life.

Red died a few days later. The details surrounding exactly what kind of "accident" happened that evening on the banks of the mighty Zambezi River died with him. When I received the call from my Mum that he was dead I cried heartily. Red was an exceptional friend and to this day I miss him.

I spent much of the rest of that day on the phone, speaking with friends back home, remembering Red, and slowly but surely, my attention shifted from Red and focused on me and I realized how I'd been pretty pathetic lately. I was alive. I was married to someone I loved. I was living in the United States of America, this incredible land of opportunity. Once again, I accepted that I was the sum of my choices; I was exactly who, what and where I chose to be. That night, I went and sat in a church and said "Thank-you" to Red. I thanked him for the gift of his friendship while he was alive, for the memories that I would always treasure and for the truth he had helped me realize that day; I was alive and it was time for me to get on with living.

Getting Going Again

After a series of tests, my lung doctor prescribed some medicine that didn't go so well with alcohol. I then decided, with the support of some anonymous friends, to stop drinking. It was awesome. The breathing medicine worked the way it was meant to. I seemed to annoy and disappoint Carrie a lot less, and little by little, the excitement and ambition that had seeped out of my life crept back in.

Early one morning after Carrie had set off to work, I sat down at our tired, round wooden kitchen table with a pencil, a blank notepad and a pot full of hot coffee. I began scribbling some notes and questions that I couldn't get out of my head. What did I want my new life in this new land to look like? How was I going to get from the life I was living to the life I wanted? I didn't yet know the answers.

Fortunately, while describing my difficulty to Sean, one of my new American friends, he suggested that I think about the kind of people I wanted to hang out with. He suggested I picture the faces and write down the names of a few people who I liked and respected, and then write down what it was I liked and respected about how they lived their lives.

As I worked on my list, I soon discovered that the people I liked and respected were people who loved living their lives. Some of them were incredibly successful financially and others were not. Some were incredibly successful professionally and others were not. Some had blissfully happy marriages and happy families and some did not.

However, they each seemed to be comfortable in their own skin. They gave themselves the permission and freedom to dream up the lives they wanted and then went and lived them. When they stumbled, they admitted that they messed up. They all seemed to be authentic human beings who lived with integrity and dignity, and as far as I could see, they were morally and spiritually sound. It didn't take me long to figure out that their lives were filled with peace, joy and success because their thoughts, words and actions were aligned. I noticed that I liked being around those people; I liked how I felt about myself when I hung out with them and the sense of ambition and confidence they evoked in me. As Sean often reminded me, "Show me your friends and I'll show you your future."

I figured out what I wanted my new life in this new land to look like. I wanted that elusive sense of peace that comes with being comfortable in my own skin. I wanted to be physically and emotionally healthy. I wanted to make a lot of money. I wanted a nice big house and nice stuff. I wanted a gaggle of healthy, happy children and a wonderful marriage to a sexy wife who liked me and was proud of me. I wanted to make a contribution to society. I wanted world peace and I wanted thinner thighs. I wanted the peace that comes from a true relationship with God and the joy that comes from a true appreciation of life.

Now I had to figure out how I was going to travel from the life I was living to the life that I wanted to lead. I looked at what I was doing and how I was doing it. It was clear that thinking the same way, making the same choices, doing the same things, just wasn't going to take me to where I wanted to go. Doc Ncube's words came back to me ... one day back in Mater Dei Hospital when I'd been feeling particularly sorry for myself, he'd urged me to remember that I was the sum of my choices and that I was exactly who, what and where I chose to be in life.

At the time I hadn't been all that impressed with what he had to say. I remember thinking how easy it was for him to stand there sharing his fortune cookie wisdom with me. It wasn't him lying on the bed with bits and pieces missing. Even though I knew that he was probably right, I wasn't anywhere near ready to admit that. I wasn't ready to accept and take responsibility for my life; it was far easier for me just to blame everyone and everything for all of the bad things that had happened to me. Now, a few years later, his words sunk in and I realized that I needed to start making smarter choices if I wanted to live a better life.

Once again, I took an honest-to-goodness look at my life and how I was living it. I thought that I'd found a way to keep one foot in Africa and the other in America by importing and then selling African art. It was a great idea and it may have worked really well for someone else, but not for me. It was similar to when years ago, I'd been surrounded by real soldiers; I'd realized that I wasn't cut out to be a soldier. It was when I was surrounded by real artists that I realized I wasn't cut out for a career in the art world either. I still have an incredible collection of African works of art that I never sold.

The night that I learnt that I was not cut out for a career in the art world was the night that I'd been invited to show some of my pieces at an art exhibition at a prestigious little art gallery. The evening was a lot of fun. I spent it munching on hors d'oevres, draining champagne flutes filled to the brim with ice cold sparkling water and hugging and air-kissing the most darling, eclectic folks I'd ever come across. The night was a huge success and for me, the highlight of the evening was after the exhibition when some of my new colleagues took me out for a late dinner to celebrate. I had new colleagues because I'd found a new career. More precisely, it found me.

One night a few months earlier, Carrie came home from a long shift at the hospital. I could tell that she was exhausted as she collapsed onto our oversized couch. She looked across the room to where I was "working on the computer". Then, speaking with a very calm blend of resignation, sorrow and determination, she said "You need to find a job tomorrow or you need to move out." She'd reached the end of her rope.

My days supposedly spent working to launch my art import company were leading me nowhere. Carrie was sick and tired of being broke. She was sick and tired of me being miserable, and of wondering what had happened to the man she'd fallen in love with and married. Honestly, I was relieved that it had come to a head. More than once in the last few weeks, I found myself in my car fighting the urge to head to the airport and board a flight from this life to anywhere outside America; but I didn't leave. I loved Carrie with all of my heart, and I wondered if I loved her so much, why would I spend so much time disappointing and hurting her?

The next morning I showed up at an employment agency. I spoke to one of the associates and told her that I needed a job that day. Looking at my resume, she told me that it might take a while to find a suitable placement. I asked her what she had starting the next day. That afternoon, I went to the grocery store and brought the ingredients for one of Carrie's favorite meals, a pasta dish with a marinara sauce and some garlic bread. That night, I cooked Carrie dinner and the next morning I set off for my new job.

I started working in a call center covering the shifts that no one else wanted. I never actually got to do the job I'd been placed for because during my training, the manager decided that my skills would be better used elsewhere. I was grateful for the opportunities that came my way and I made the most of them. I quickly climbed the ladder, earning more and more responsibility and slowly and surely, rebuilding my self-esteem and rekindling my relationship with Carrie.

One day, the chap who ran the agency that had placed me in my current position came in to visit his client. As I passed by the office, I noticed that he was sitting there alone. I knocked on the door, and not waiting for a response, I entered.

"You don't know me. My name is Paul Templer and your company placed me here a few months ago. Here is my resume. Once you've looked at it, I think you'll agree that you could be making more money off me. If you know of any opportunities you think I'd be suited to, please don't hesitate to recommend me."

He looked at me, as if to say, "Do you know who I am and who you are? I own this company and you work in the call center!" Nonetheless, he took my resume, smiled and said, "Sure." The next day, he called. He had set up a meeting with some people he thought I might find interesting. He was right.

At the meeting, I received a glimpse into a world that I'd always suspected existed but until then, I had no idea how to gain admittance to. It was a world populated by doctors, lawyers, philosophers, economists, engineers and entrepreneurs, academics, adventurers, soldiers and athletes. It was the world of Professional Coaching. I was incredibly fortunate that, though lacking any formal education in the field, the people I met with that day thought I had potential and so they hired and then trained me.

The work I do as a coach is most heavily influenced by the works of Fernando Flores and Dr. Peter Yaholkovsky in language and action, Richard Strozzi-Heckler in Somatic Leadership, biologists Humberto Maturana and Francisco Varela, continental philosopher Martin Heidegger and linguist John Searle. This all comes together to form the foundation of Ontological Coaching and Commitment Based Management.

As days bled into weeks and months into years, my competence as a coach, process designer and the number of miles in my frequent flyer account grew enormously. It didn't seem to matter much whether it was in the world of finance or manufacturing, distribution or retail, insurance or health care, the one thing all organizations seemed to have in common was that people got up in the morning and went to work, spoke to each other and coordinated with each other to get things done. If people wanted to do so more effectively and their organizations were committed to functioning as high-performing teams, I could help.

Coincidentally, as my professional life blossomed, my home life improved dramatically too. Carrie was relieved that I'd found something to do that I loved. She wasn't the only one concerned that given the life I'd lived in Africa, I might not have been able to find something to do in America that got my juices flowing.

Carrie and I often marvel at how in one lifetime, I've run safaris both in the jungle and in the business world. It turns out that leading clients on safari is not that different from working with people in the business world. In both the African and the corporate jungles, success or failure is often determined by how nicely people can play together; how well they can manage the mood of their interactions so that they can communicate and coordinate effectively, build trust, innovate and get stuff done.

Chapter 8

A More Challenging Adventure

Picture Perfect
Spring 2001

After a while, Carrie and I bought our first house. It was a cute little brick bungalow on a tree-lined street. Our house quickly became our home. I tore up the carpet, refinished the floors, stripped wallpaper and painted walls while Carrie decorated and made it feel like our own. Elsa and Shumba, our two lion hunting Rhodesian Ridgeback dogs, completed the first in a series of pictures I'd dreamt of back when I was deciding what I wanted my new life in this new land to look like. I had a wife whom I adored and who, for the most part, was quite fond of me. I had a career that I loved that was taking off. Carrie and I were both working and were able to pay our bills and I had two dogs that went nuts every time I arrived home.

Tony Filippis

After a few years, traveling for work all the time began to wear on me. The weekdays passed in a blur as every moment was filled coaching, designing and mobilizing new processes; all of which involved meeting, interacting with, and learning from some incredibly talented colleagues and clients. Carrie was working full time too and it got to where we only saw each other on our weekends and vacations. Not that we were complaining. We were grateful for the opportunities that had come our way and were slowly and surely getting ourselves in a position to grow our family.

One day, I was having lunch with my dear friend and mentor, Tony Filippis. I was telling him that I felt pretty guilty for neglecting Make-A-Difference of late. He quickly stopped my whining and offered that if I was really serious about making a difference, I needed to first take care of myself and my family. Only then would I be able to commit and focus the time, energy and attention needed to take my foundation to the next level.

I accepted, pro bono, various invitations to speak at Metro Detroit area fundraising events and was very grateful for these opportunities. They gave me a chance to gain some speaking experience as well as promote Make-A-Difference. I was also happy to discover that when I spoke, it was usually pretty well received. As Carrie and I were intending to one day raise a family, the prospect of me being on the road five days a week, every week as our children grew up, didn't sound good to either of us. As much as I loved the work I was doing and enjoyed the company of the people I was working with, I knew that for it to remain a treasured part of what I did and who I was, I needed to stop and look at my situation as it really was. When I did, it became clear that it was time to design what was to happen next.

Working with Richard Farrell, my longtime coach, friend and collaborative thinker, it quickly became obvious that paying some of my bills as a professional speaker was an option. Equally obvious was that if I chose to follow that path, I needed to do a lot of work before I quit my day job.

I entered the National Speakers Association's twenty-month

ProTrack program. It was an intensive and exhaustive program, especially while working full time. But, I was appreciative of being able to work with a group of well established and highly regarded Certified Speaking Professionals who graciously and effectively introduced me and the rest of my group to every aspect of professional speaking. It turned out that there was a lot more to being a professional speaker and successfully navigating the speaking world than I first thought.

Katelyn Rose and a Consulting Career

Meanwhile, Carrie and I welcomed our beautiful, happy, healthy daughter, Katelyn Rose into the world in April 2003. The day she was born was both the happiest and most overwhelming day of my life to date.

I'd resigned, effective that month, from the consulting company I'd been working with for the last few years as I didn't want to be on the road five days a week anymore.

Thank goodness for Carrie's mom Joan, who came and helped us when we brought Katelyn home. I was no use to anyone. I disappeared into my basement office for days. The plan I'd designed and embarked upon seemed like a far better idea when it was just Carrie and me. Now that we had a new baby, the whole world looked very different. A few days prior, I was ambitious, well prepared, confident and committed to our family's future as I launched my new speaking and coaching business. I was going to pay my bills, make a difference, and spend time with my family. Now, with a baby, all I could think about was how irresponsible I was to quit my job at a time like this.

A few years earlier, upon completion of my formal training, the coaches who'd introduced me to this new world had presented me with a scroll. On it was written a quotation by William H. Murray, the leader of The Scottish Himalayan Expedition.

"Until one is committed, there is hesitancy, the chance to draw back, always ineffectiveness. Concerning all acts of initiative (and creation), there is one elementary truth the ignorance of which kills countless ideas and splendid plans; that the moment one definitely commits oneself, then providence moves too. A whole stream of events issues from the decision, raising in one's favor all manner of unforeseen incidents, meetings and material assistance, which no man could have dreamt would have come his way. I learned a deep respect for one of Goethe's couplets:

Whatever you can do or dream you can, begin it.

Boldness has genius, power and magic in it!"

I kept this quote handy and read it often, particularly when I found myself wavering.

On the Make-A-Difference front, one event stands out in my mind from that year. Ossur Engineering, a large prosthetic manufacturer, donated over half a million dollars worth of artificial legs to Make-A-Difference and we were able to ratchet up our support to programs in Africa. It was a real privilege to be able to facilitate that transaction. I was incredibly grateful both for the contents of the donation and the demonstration of kindness and care that people had for each other. Today, nameless, faceless folks in Africa are getting another shot at life. They're able to walk around and get on with their lives because some people in Michigan U.S.A. cared enough to expend the effort to make a donation.

I completed the ProTrack program and was spending a lot of time getting out there in front of audiences developing and practicing my speaking. Many times before I climbed on stage, I'd wonder what in the heck I was doing. In an American survey, the fear of public speaking ranked above the fear of death, prompting comedian Jerry Seinfeld's speculation that, at a funeral, most of us would rather be lying in the coffin than reading the eulogy. My fear of speaking is alive and well.

However, once I'm standing in front of an audience, my fear goes away and is replaced with gratitude towards the people who are taking the time to listen. I'm grateful to whoever decides to sign the checks to allow me to speak. I'm grateful that my experiences entertain, inspire and motivate people to take action.

I even motivated myself to take a new kind of action. I began to train for a marathon. I was relieved as I discovered that my newly reconstructed left foot was up to training. About a year earlier, the surgeon had reconstructed bits of it that hadn't worked so well after being crushed by the hippo. I had hoped that would be my last hippo related surgery. Given that I now had two feet that worked and I could run, I thought "Why not run a marathon?" It was something that had never appealed to me before, but as a one-armed man with a reconstructed foot, I knew I could do it, so I did.

At the mile twenty-four marker, as I gulped down a cup of Gatorade and chased it with a gulp of water, old women and young boys seemed to effortlessly pass me by, but I just smiled. Watching me jog by with that vacant smile on my face, an observer would have been forgiven for thinking that maybe completing the marathon was going to be too much for me; maybe I'd lost my mind. I was exhausted, but mostly I was thinking about all of the experiences that had brought me to this point.

With the benefit of hindsight, it seemed to me that each event in my life and how I'd responded to it prepared me for the next. It seemed that when I was able to get out of my own way, accept what was going on, and not take myself too seriously, I would find plenty of opportunities to learn and grow. At the same time, I could see that when I assumed accountability and responsibility for my actions, I could live in a wonderful world, no matter my present circumstances. I could experience the peace of God and joy in my life.

At the end of the marathon, Carrie and six-month old Katelyn were there to congratulate me. I was so happy to see them and so grateful for

all that they were to me and my life. At the same time, I got a glimpse of
the price they paid for loving me. I was the sum of my choices; I was who,
what and where I chose to be in life, but it seemed that when convenient,
I chose to be blind to what my choices cost others.

My training for the marathon cost everyone in that it required a
major time commitment. I spent time running instead of helping Carrie
with the baby. I expected people to build their lives around my choices. I
needed to be more careful. Unchecked, this kind of behavior could have
wound up hurting the people I loved and cared about the most.

Wanting to raise my game in the speaking world even higher,
I went to a National Speakers Association Workshop. I figured that
if I was serious about performing at a high level, surrounding myself
with experienced speakers for a few days would be a great learning
opportunity. Jane Atkinson, speaker launcher to the stars, presented
one of the breakout sessions I attended. She spoke about the mutually
beneficial relationship that could and should exist between speakers and
speaker bureaus. According to the checklist she handed out, I was years
away from being ready to work with speaker bureaus. That wasn't news
to me. I knew that as a professional speaker I was deficient in so many
areas, but Jane excited me, because now I understood why.

I crafted a letter to Jane that included the filled out checklist, and
sent it to her.

*According to the standards you presented at the recent workshop, I am years
away from being ready to work with speaker bureaus, and further still from
being in condition to work with you.*

*I'm committed to entertaining, producing value and making a difference
to the people who listen to what I have to say. I am committed to succeeding in
this business.*

*As a safari guide and business coach, I've learned that when I'm traveling
through the jungle – it makes no difference if it's in the African outdoors*

surrounded by wild animals or if I'm in the corporate boardrooms, offices and cubicles surrounded by human beings – if I'm with someone who knows what they're doing, it makes for a more enjoyable and productive adventure.

Can we speak to see if there is some way we can work together?

We spoke, and Jane and I started working together. Financially, it was going to be a challenge but I felt it was an incredible investment for my family's future. Much to our financial planner's chagrin, we cashed out our life savings, retirement plans and ran up our credit cards. I was still doing some coaching and process design work and when I wasn't doing that, I was out speaking, shooting a demo video, building a website, branding materials, marketing myself and doing my best to launch a successful professional speaking career.

Carrie and I welcomed our second healthy and happy daughter, Erin, into the world about eighteen months after Katelyn had arrived. We couldn't have been happier. Erin was a gorgeous baby. She was laid back and had a smile that could light up a city block.

Though financially stretched, Carrie and I definitely saw a light at the end of the tunnel and it didn't seem to be a train. I was getting paid more and more for speaking engagements and our financial planner seemed relieved as we were still on track to pay off our debt. There were a few speaker bureaus that had agreed to work with me, but most of my business at that point came from repeat clients and word of mouth. Slowly but surely, my business was evolving and taking off. I felt like I had the best of all worlds. I had a burgeoning professional career as a coach and a speaker, and I was healthy, happy and in love with my family.

Something Wrong with Erin

Saturday February 26th, 2005 was the night before Chris Rock hosted the 77th Annual Academy Awards. It was the night before Jamie

Foxx won best actor in *Ray* and Hilary Swank won the best actress award for her performance in *Million Dollar Baby*.

Carrie and I had been out for an early dinner with some friends. We'd taken the girls with us. We enjoyed fine fare, exceptional company and delightful conversation. Everyone was having a wonderful evening. To me, that was about as good as it got. As I drove us home in our minivan, my tummy was full and I was about as content as a man could be.

Carrie was in the back with the girls. "There's something going on with Erin … Never mind, it's probably nothing." Her tone belied her words. As a mother and a nurse, I knew that Carrie was hyper vigilant when it came to the kids. Given her background in nursing, she had a different set of distinctions and saw the world through different eyes than I did. When we got home, Erin seemed fine and everyone went to bed.

The next night, just before the Oscars started, Erin did it again. It was her eyes. Ever so briefly, they shot up and to the side and her body shuddered. Then she was fine again. As parents, we didn't really want to acknowledge what had happened. "Babies jerk, right? That's normal?" Carrie nodded, half-heartedly attempting to smile before setting up an appointment with the pediatrician.

The pediatrician ran a neurological test and everything seemed fine. To be on the safe side, the doc set up an appointment with a pediatric neurologist. The pediatric neurologist ran more tests and then declared that she was fine. There was nothing for us to worry about, but driving home, she did "it" again. We called the pediatric neurologist back and she said to take Erin to the Emergency Room at the nearest hospital.

At the hospital, Erin underwent more tests including a routine CT scan. "It's just part of our normal protocol," the ER doc assured us. "We are crossing our t's and dotting our i's."

A little while later, he came back and told us that he was going to prescribe some anti-seizure meds for her and that we should follow up with the pediatric neurologist. A little while later, he came back. This time his demeanor was different as he asked us to follow him into a little room with a tiny screen with pictures and Erin's name on it. Then he showed us the picture and pointed to the tumor on her brain.

We took her from the ER up to her room in the hospital. A phone call to Carrie's dad ensured that Katelyn was okay and would be taken care of and Carrie and I spent much of the night speaking to doctors and nurses as we tried to grasp the ungraspable.

I left Carrie at the hospital that night and sitting at home while Katelyn slept, I cried and swore, and then I pulled myself together. I took a few deep breaths and I knew that I had to stop my mind from racing. I had to look at our situation as it really was. If I let myself get caught up and carried away by the story, I wasn't going to be of any use to anyone – not to Carrie, not to Erin and not to Katelyn.

I needed to come up with a plan.

First things first, I needed to take care of Katelyn Rose. Just coming up on her second birthday, she knew that there was something going on and that it wasn't good. Carrie's dad, Charlie, stepped up to the plate and coordinated with the rest of the family to take care of Katelyn – which was no small task given that Joan, Carrie's mom, had just had a car crash and was not doing well.

Then, I cleared my calendar for the next few weeks. I gave clients as much of a heads-up as I could and took care of all concerns there and then.

I made the calls to family to let them know what was going on and set up a process for keeping them all in the loop. Then, I reached out. In addition to the support that I knew I would receive from my family, I knew that I needed some help keeping my head straight. I connected with my coach Richard, my friend Sean and my medical insurance broker Brian and asked for their help.

Next, I packed a bag and went back to the hospital. It was going to be a long few days and my body and my attention needed to be there for Carrie and for Erin. Carrie was holding up as well as could be expected. She truly was a superstar. For the umpteenth time, I thanked the Lord that she was my wife and that she was the mother of my children. The way she was moving through this nightmare with such dignity both filled and broke my heart.

That morning, we met with a new pediatric neurologist and a neurological surgeon and more doctors and more nurses representing more pediatric specialties and sub-specialties than I knew existed. That was a day filled with tests and waiting. My friend Sean took the day off and came and sat with us. Not only is he a good man and a true friend, he's also a dentist. His objectivity and ability to help us decipher some of the medical jargon was invaluable. Even more useful was his presence, his love and his support.

As the minutes turned into hours, the hours turned into days. As the results from the tests started coming in, a picture started to emerge. At first, things looked pretty grim. A brain tumor in a three and a half month old baby is awful news, but then we got a glimmer of hope. It was possible that the tumor was benign. We would keep an eye on it and come back for more tests in three months time. Maybe things weren't going to be so bad after all. Maybe Erin was going to be okay. All we had to do was get Erin's seizures under control and then we could be discharged from the hospital.

On Friday morning, Erin's situation in the hospital seemed stable as we waited for the results of the last few tests and looked for medicine to control her seizures. No babysitters were available that morning so I took Katelyn with me to a friend's funeral. I turned my phone off during the service. As I turned it back on, my heart sank. There were a lot of messages.

The neurological surgeon had taken the results of Erin's tests before the tumor board and based on the information they had, the tumor was malignant and it needed to come out as soon as was possible. The surgeon wanted to transfer Erin to the nearby Children's Hospital immediately. Carrie couldn't get ahold of me and things were starting to move way too fast. After speaking to her pediatrician, she told the doc that she was going to wait for a second opinion.

The weekend was a blur. We had to get the test results hand delivered to another hospital's tumor board, which had agreed to review Erin's case first thing Monday morning. We were busy returning calls to family and friends and Erin's seizures were happening more often and getting progressively worse. When she wasn't seizing, she looked at us with her deep blue eyes as if to ask, "What's going on? Please stop it!"

When our eyes connected she'd pause and give off a radiant smile. When the doc dropped by on Saturday night to check up on Erin, she saw that Erin had more than forty seizures so far that day. She impressed upon us the urgency of the situation and the next morning, an ambulance transferred Carrie and Erin to Children's Hospital.

Moving into a hospital with a very ill child onto a ward filled with a lot of other very ill children was an eye-opening experience. As parents, we all had very little in common – some of us were wealthy and some weren't. Some children had a mom and a dad and some had neither. Some children were getting better, but others didn't have much time. We were different races, colors, cultures, religions and creeds, but none of this mattered because as parents, we had some important things in common; our children were sick, suffering and scared and at times, we felt helpless, and nothing else mattered as much as being there for our children.

On Tuesday, we were moved to another room where Erin was hooked up to yet another machine with all kinds of wires attached to her head – she rolled over that day for the very first time and was so very impressed with herself. There were a few more tests they needed to run, and Erin would go in for surgery the next morning.

That night was undoubtedly the longest, darkest night of my life. Carrie and I took turns trying, for the most part unsuccessfully, to get some sleep. They say you'll never find an atheist in a foxhole – I don't know about that, but I do know that as I said a rosary I begged, pleaded, bargained, promised anything and everything. "Please just let my little girl live and please stop her suffering."

Erin turned four months old on Wednesday, March 9th, 2005. By the time the sun came up, our day was well underway as Erin went through her final test. The result was at first encouraging. It seemed that the mass on her brain was most likely benign. That was where the good news ended. The doc told us that it still needed to come out and it needed to happen that day. I glanced up to the heavens and asked for guidance "Thy will be done."

I looked at Carrie, marveling at how incredible she was as she continued to move with dignity and grace. "Tell us more…" she invited. Their plan was to go in and remove the cyst. While they had her open, they were going to test the brain and see if they could find the diseased areas that were sparking her seizures. We were warned that there might be a scenario where they would leave her brain open to run some more tests and go back in.

"What's the prognosis?" I asked.

"Good," the doctor replied, "if we get the mass it will probably stop the seizures and we can expect a full recovery."

"What are the risks?" I doubled back." He paused and replied, "She could die, be permanently brain damaged, there's always the chance of a stroke…" The list went on.

We went as far as we could into the pre-op room with Erin and then kissed her goodbye and promised that we'd be waiting for her when she woke up. That was the worst moment of my life.

Carrie and I were warned that the surgery would take a while. We ate some pretty unremarkable cafeteria food, a slice of pizza, a bottle of water and eight hours later, Erin was still in surgery and we were still sitting waiting. As the day passed by, I watched all of the other parents as they came and went. It didn't seem to matter if the person's child was having an ingrown toenail removed, their tonsils out, or even the one mother whose son was having his third open-heart surgery – this was one of the very last places in the world that any of us wanted to be.

As I sat there, I said my rosary and had a conversation with God. I was trying to read a book called *Who lives, who dies and why?* but I really couldn't stay focused. Carrie and I chatted occasionally, but mostly we just sat quietly together with our thoughts.

A friend of Carrie's showed up to offer us her support. She was a widow who had raised five children on her own. Judy Ann had recently become a nun and then more recently, had gone off on her own to work with terminally ill children and their families. It didn't matter to Judy Anne who the kids were or where the kids came from, what their parents did or didn't do. Her calling in this world was to do what she could to help those who needed her most. Her presence there was a gift that we'll always be grateful for.

Carrie's dad came to sit with us too in that surreal little waiting room. Then, the surgeon came through to speak to us. It had been a long surgery he said. They'd managed to get the entire tumor and it was in fact benign. He told us that there had been a lot of seizure activity coming from all over her little brain and that they'd taken out the most diseased part of her brain but they hadn't got it all because of the risk. Also, because she was so little, they'd decided against leaving her open with the grids attached and had in fact closed her up. He told us that if we wanted to see her, we should rush in as they were wheeling her up to the pediatric intensive care unit.

She lay there unconscious, her tiny body fighting for life, being monitored and kept alive by humming machines and loving, caring people. Erin's face and body relaxed, full of peace and acceptance.

I sat alone with my thoughts. I had no tears left. I had no rage left. I didn't know if I had anything left. I didn't know if it was possible for me to feel more helpless and I didn't even have the energy to feel sorry for myself about that. My little girl was either going to live or she was going to die, and aside from continuing to beg God for a miracle, there wasn't a damned thing that I could do about it, so I begged. I prayed and I did what I could to support Carrie and our other beautiful daughter, Katelyn.

Carrie dealt with more than anyone should ever have to. On top of everything that was going on with Erin, her mom Joan, while recovering from her car crash and feeling poorly, had discovered that her body was riddled with cancer. She was terminally ill, and only had weeks left to live.

The physical and emotional demands upon Carrie were diabolical; when she wasn't at the hospital comforting Erin, she was spending time with and taking care of her mom whose condition was deteriorating day by day. Every time I look back at those dark days and darker nights, I remember the way Carrie gave of herself without ever asking for anything in return. When I remember the incredible love, comfort and support that she brought to all those around her, freely offering her quiet strength, I'm overwhelmed with pride and love for the gift that she is.

Erin wasn't doing well at all. If she lived, who knew what her future held? In addition to taking out the tumor and a part of her brain, the doctors told us that they thought she might have had a stroke while she was undergoing surgery. Days and nights blended into each other slogging by one second at a time. The original prognosis was gone.

There was a marked increase in the frequency and severity of her seizures, and when she was seizing, those were the only times that she really showed any evidence of life.

The prognosis became, "We'll just have to wait and see." Before long, we were discharged from the hospital and urged to get on with life. At that time, Erin's condition was declared to be intractable, meaning that she didn't respond in the way we hoped she would to any of the medication she was taking for the seizures. We took a few deep breaths, looked up to the heavens and prepared for more.

One Sunday night, Erin's seizures got to be particularly scary. They were coming hard and fast, not really letting up in between. Once again, I was incredibly grateful that Carrie was a nurse as we pinned Erin's tiny body down and gave her the emergency treatments that her doctor had cautiously prescribed, "to use only in case of an emergency." I called him to let him know what was going on. Once I'd described her symptoms, in a sad and disappointed voice, he pronounced that her condition had evolved and that she now had Infantile Spasms.

My stomach turned and my heart sank. This was the prognosis that we'd dreaded. "At least it isn't Infantile Spasms," we'd often comforted each other.

As we understood it, Infantile Spasms is terminal for one in five children afflicted. The statistics said that eighty percent of those who survived would be severely physically and mentally disabled. That's what the statistics said. Mark Twain quoted the British politician, Benjamin Disraeli as saying, "There are three kinds of lies: lies, damned lies and statistics." That was the view I was going to take; Erin wasn't a statistic. She was my daughter and for as long as there was any time left on the game clock, I was going to do everything that I could to help her.

After we stabilized Erin, Carrie went to spend the night with her mom. As my two beautiful girls slept quietly and my two large dogs snored noisily, I caught up on mail. One of the envelopes I opened was from the John Bradburne Trust, a group dedicated to helping Lepers in Africa. They were a group I supported both personally and, because the lepers were amputees, we were able to support them through our Foundation.

As I glanced through the newsletter, there was a note welcoming Anne Lander to the organization. My heart stopped as the words "Anne Lander" jumped out at me. My fingers flew across my laptop's keyboard as I composed a note. I needed to find out if this was the same Anne Lander who had impacted my life all those years ago when I was the one suffering in the hospital.

"Yes Paul, of course I remember you." It was Anne. I brought her up to speed regarding Erin's condition and asked for her help. I wanted her to fix Erin. She said that fixing Erin was something that she couldn't do and suggested instead that we focus on praying for acceptance of the situation as it was. I was devastated. The glimmer of hope that had suddenly and unexpectedly flared up was just as quickly extinguished. I'd wanted Anne to say "Sure I'll fix her." She would have then had a quick chat with the chap upstairs and "Voila!" Erin would be healed. Instead, I had to pray for acceptance to this God who I thought was doing a pretty lousy job at the time.

For Erin's sake, I was willing to do anything. I had quite a few interesting and raw conversations with the chap upstairs. I had quite a bit to say to Him about this notion that he was a loving God. I told Him how I really wasn't getting it and how I was more than just a little pissed at Him. I went through the bargaining phase. "Fix her and take me instead."

With Anne's loving support, I was able to work through much of my frustration, resentment, fear and anger to a place where the beginnings of acceptance and gratitude started to show up. I developed acceptance for the situation as it was and gratitude for all of the possibilities that still existed.

We had concerns with the medicines that we could get our hands on in the United States. They weren't working for Erin. That said, we'd discovered that though not FDA approved, there was a drug available in Canada that might help. A doctor in Canada prescribed the drug and for a while, her seizures seemed to be slowing down.

A week or two later, Katelyn had her second birthday party at Grandma's house. The whole family came to celebrate. That night Grandma Joan died. She was a good person who lived with integrity and died with dignity. The world is poorer for her passing and richer for her having been here.

The next week was a nightmare. Front and center, there was Joan's funeral and everything that went with it. Erin's seizures were getting worse again. I was leaving for Africa at the end of the week to do some work on a documentary about hippos with National Geographic.

"How could I even consider leaving at a time like this?" That was the question that some people asked me to my face, while most asked behind my back. When directly asked, I usually answered, "It's a fabulous opportunity that will increase our ability to pay our bills in the future."

In conversation with Anne, we'd come up with a game plan for Erin's seizures. It was quite straightforward, given my crazy schedule and the five-hour time difference that existed between London, England and Detroit, Michigan. We decided that at four o'clock in the morning my time, Anne, her friend Pamela and a whole bunch of other folks, most of whom I'll never know, would focus our attention and our prayers on Erin.

The plan was simple. We would link up at the prescribed time and would hold the healing focus for approximately twenty minutes. I was to keep my hand about an inch or slightly more above Erin's little head, relax, let go and let God work His wonder of love and healing. We did it two mornings in a row. On the first, I'm embarrassed to admit that I let "relax" become "fall back to sleep".

The next morning was something altogether different. As I lay there, my hand hovering above the bulging snake-like scar that crawled over much of one side of her head, I felt this incredible warmth starting to build in the space between us; I moved my hand and the temperature dropped dramatically. I moved my hand back and the warmth returned and it wasn't just between my hand and her head. It was filling me in much the same way that it did years ago when Anne laid her hands on me and prayed for healing. It was that same sense and familiar warmth of peace that had filled me years earlier when I was sloshing at the bottom of the blood filled canoe, and with my broken and torn body, I had chosen to live.

Erin's seizures never went away completely, but for the next few weeks as life and death crowded in all around us, Erin experienced peace as the frequency and severity of her seizures eased off significantly.

We buried Joan, and as Carrie came to terms with the loss of her mother, I left to go and work for a few weeks in Africa. When I returned, so did Erin's seizures.

We were running out of options when Erin's doctor recommended ACTH – hormonal therapy with steroids. It had a list as long as my arm of really unpleasant possible side effects including congestive heart failure and death. No one ever said that being a parent was going to be easy, but sometimes I thought our experience bordered on ridiculous. We had a sick daughter with a potentially fatal diagnosis who was not responding to any medicines, and one of the few remaining options could kill her. That said – I knew that I had choices.

I didn't have to go with the ACTH. There were other "alternative" therapies that we hadn't tried yet. There was also the option of choosing to have faith that God would take care of her. I blinked, I lost my nerve and we agreed to the ACTH. Erin experienced no negative side effects and after having one last major cluster of intense, bone-shaking, teeth-clenching seizures, they went away.

Day by day and breath by breath, life began to creep back into Erin's little body and our baby started to live again. The little changes unnoticeable to most, were huge to us.

"Did you see the glimmer of life in her eyes?"

"She looked at me, I swear."

"She smiled at me with her eyes."

Days bled into weeks and weeks into months and months into years, and one blessing blossomed into another, each as beautiful as the one before. "She smiled at me… She moved… She rolled over… She lifted her head… She sat up… She crawled… She walked."

Erin and her faithful sidekick Carrie journeyed through their new adventure with gratitude and acceptance that I sometimes struggled to wrap my head around. Carrie was incredible – a fierce protector, committed advocate, patient teacher, diligent taskmaster, joyful playmate and loving mother. The two of them never complained. Instead, they seemed to draw strength from each other.

Attached to Preferences

Prior to this, no one would have accused me of being a "fixer". But I suddenly found myself trying to fix Erin. The Third Chinese Patriarch, Seng-ts'an says in his Verses on the Faith-Mind, "The Great Way is not difficult for those not attached to preferences."

This may well be true. In fact, I believe it to be so. That said, I was totally hooked into my preference that Erin be fixed, and I was oblivious to the effect this had on the lives of the people I claimed to love, particularly Erin, Carrie and Katelyn.

I wasn't taking the time to be there for them. My body was there, but my mind was far, far away. I didn't really listen to what they had to say. I didn't look into their eyes or connect with what they were feeling. I missed out on the opportunities to share a much needed hug, cook the occasional meal, play in the park, go for a walk, read stories, say prayers, or hang out and connect as a husband and a dad. Instead, my attention was focused on what was wrong with Erin and what needed to be done to fix her. For a while, I became obsessed, poring over the internet all hours of the day and night, learning all I could about her condition and how to solve it.

Hours turned into days, days into weeks and weeks into months. In March of 2007, Jack Merson Templer arrived. Weighing in at eight pounds and four ounces with a head full of dark hair, piercing blue eyes and strong healthy lungs, he quickly made himself right at home. As the only person in Erin's life who sees her without limitations, and blessed with the heart of a lion and the unbridled optimism of a beloved toddler, Jack dragged us laughing back into the light.

Normalcy was returning. I was speaking a lot and coaching for Chris Majer, leader of The Human Potential Project. Chris' clients have included professional athletes, the military (including projects with some of the U.S. Special Forces, the Navy SEALs and the Green Berets) and corporations around the world. The Human Potential Project produces incredible results when it comes to optimal performance with both individuals and teams. I thoroughly enjoyed working with him and his team, helping people to lead their organizations more effectively and profitably with integrity and dignity.

opusdynamic
January 2011

I will always appreciate the support Chris gave me when I took a leap of faith starting opusdynamic, my own consulting company. Taking Chris' advice, I surrounded myself with people who are a lot smarter than I am and along with my business partners, Patrick and Kyle, and a team of committed and extremely competent colleagues, we've gone on to build a successful global enterprise that includes consulting, logistics, multi-media and IT development companies all focused on being profitable, socially responsible and making a positive difference in people's lives.

With some stability on the professional front and given our life experiences, Make-A- Difference evolved. I realized I needed to make some changes if it were to grow. I began to create a new board to lead us into the future. My new board pointed out that though my intentions were good, we needed to refocus if we were really committed to making a difference. Along with our mission, our name changed.

Nowadays it's called The Templer Foundation and we continue to provide support for disabled and terminally ill children as well as collaborating on the frontlines in the treatment of Post Traumatic Stress Disorder. We're gratefully promoting social enterprise initiatives in support of urban renewal, sustainable economic development, health, nutrition, and human services, and education and training – all in support of people living with dignity.

Erin is still with us. She's a miracle. You know what – she inspires me every single day as she faces each day's challenges head on without complaint. She's my daily reminder that adversity doesn't build character insomuch as it reveals it. And as long as I can keep that in mind, whenever I look at what's left of me, it's clear that though I lost my fight with that rogue hippo, I won my life.

Epilogue

With Erin's challenges, we aren't always sure what will happen next. However, we are sure that we're incredibly blessed to have one another.

Carrie and I agree that as a husband and wife who brought children into the world, we are responsible for taking care of them. We know that taking care of them includes taking care of each other. We strive to always speak lovingly to one another and communicate honestly and authentically. We hope that as our kids see it, they will do the same. We strive to make our family understand that though we have very little control over much of what happens, we always have control over how we respond.

By taking care of each other one day at a time, and by always trying to do the next right thing, we have gradually built wonderful, happy lives for ourselves and our family. We are enjoying the journey and all the stops along the way.

Carrie spends her days with me, our children, our dogs, doctors, nurses, grocers, gardeners, friends, and family. I spend mine coaching and speaking in cities as far apart as Boston, Chicago, Detroit, Glasgow, London, Manchester and Miami.

The Templer Foundation continues to evolve and I continue to share my experiences and observations as a keynote speaker and coach.

I'm grateful for the opportunity to be a catalyst for productive change in people's lives as I work with high-performing individuals and teams who are committed to raising the level of their game. I get to support them in their journey to embody new competencies, find new ways to live with dignity, and to move more powerfully in their lives. Aside from spending time with my family, I can't imagine anything else I'd rather be doing.

The Silence is Deafening:

A Sermon

Very Rev. John da Costa, Anglican Dean of Salisbury, delivered a sermon at the funeral service for the victims of a terrorist attack on a civilian airplane in Rhodesia on September 3, 1978. The sentiment he expressed is deeply relevant and appropriate to today's world.

Clergymen, I am frequently told, should keep out of politics. I thoroughly agree. For this reason, I will not allow politics to be preached in this cathedral. Clergy have to be reconcilers. That is no easy job. A minister of religion who has well-known political views, and allows them to come to the fore, cannot reconcile, but will alienate others, and fail in the chief part of his ministry.

For this reason, I personally am surprised at there being two clergymen in the Executive Council. It is my sincere prayer that they can act as Christ's ambassadors of reconciliation.

My own ministry began in Ghana, where Kwame Nkrumah preached: "Seek ye first the political kingdom and all these things will be added to you." We know what became of Kwame Nkrumah. We are not to preach a political kingdom, but the kingdom of God.

Clergy are usually in the middle, shot at from both sides. It is not an enviable role. Yet times come when it is necessary to speak out in direct and forthright terms, like trumpets with unmistakable notes. I believe that this was one such time.

Nobody who holds sacred the dignity of human life can be anything but sickened at the events attending the crash of the Viscount Hunyani. Survivors have the greatest call on the sympathy and assistance of every other human being. The horror of the crash was bad enough, but that this should have been compounded by savage and treacherous murder leaves us stunned with disbelief and brings revulsion in the minds of anyone deserving the name "human."

This [atrocity], worse than anything in recent history, stinks in the nostrils of Heaven. But are we deafened with the voice of protest from nations which call themselves "civilized"? We are not. Like men in the story of the Good Samaritan, they "pass by, on the other side."

One listens for loud condemnation by Dr. David Owen* himself a medical doctor, trained to extend mercy and help to all in need.

One listens and the silence is deafening.

One listens for loud condemnation by the President of the United States,** himself a man from the Bible-Baptist belt, and again the silence is deafening.

One listens for loud condemnation by the Pope, by the Chief Rabbi, by the Archbishop of Canterbury, by all who love the name of God.

Again the silence is deafening.

I do not believe in white supremacy. I do not believe in black supremacy either. I do not believe that anyone is better than another, until he has proved himself to be so. I believe that those who govern or who seek to govern must prove themselves worthy of the trust that will be placed in them.

One looks for real leadership. One finds little in the Western world: How much less in Africa?

Who is to be blamed for this ghastly episode?

Like Pontius Pilate, the world may ask, "What is truth?" What is to be believed? That depends on what your prejudices will allow you to believe, for then no evidence will convince you otherwise.

So who is to be blamed?

First, those who fired the guns. Who were they? Youths and men who were, until recently, in church schools. This is the first terrible fact. Men who went over to the other side in a few months were so indoctrinated that all they had previously learned was obliterated. How could this happen if they had been given a truly Christian education?

Second, it is common knowledge that in large parts of the world violence is paraded on TV and cinema screens as entertainment. Films about war, murder, violence, rape, devil-possession and the like are "good box-office". Peak viewing time is set aside for murderers from Belfast, Palestine, Europe, Africa and the rest, to speak before an audience of tens of millions. Thugs are given full treatment, as if deserving respect.

Not so the victims' relations.

Who else is to be blamed?

The United Nations and their church equivalent, the W.C.C.*** I am sure they both bear blame in this. Each parade a pseudo-morality which, like all half-truths, is more dangerous than the lie direct. From the safety and comfort of New York and Geneva, high moral attitudes can safely be struck. For us in the sweat, the blood, the suffering, it is somewhat different.

Who else? The churches? Oh yes, I fear so.

For too long, too many people have been allowed to call themselves "believers" when they have been nothing of the kind. Those who believe must act. If you believe the car is going to crash, you attempt to get out. If you believe the house is on fire, you try to get help and move things quickly. If you believe a child has drunk poison, you rush him to the doctor. Belief must bring about action.

Yet churches, even in our own dangerous times, are more than half-empty all the time. We are surrounded by heathens who equate belief in God with the Western way of life. In many war areas, Africans are told to "burn their Bibles". If this call was made to us, what sort of Bibles would be handed in? Would they be dog-eared from constant use; well-thumbed and marked? Would they be pristine in their virgin loveliness, in the same box in which they were first received?

There are tens of millions of all races who call themselves believers, who never enter any house of prayer and praise. Many are folk who scream loudest against communism, yet do not themselves help to defeat these Satanic forces by means of prayer, and praise and religious witness.

For, make no mistake, if our witness were as it ought to be, men would flock to join our ranks. As it is, we are by-passed by the world, as if irrelevant.

Is anyone else to be blamed for this ghastly episode near Kariba? I think so.

Politicians throughout the world have made opportunist speeches from time to time. These add to the heap of blameworthiness, for a speech can cause wounds which may take years to heal.

The ghastliness of this ill-fated flight from Kariba will be burned upon our memories for years to come. For others, far from our borders, it is an intellectual matter, not one which affects them deeply. Here is the tragedy!

The especial danger of Marxism is its teaching that human life is cheap, expendable, of less importance than the well-being of the State. But there are men who call themselves Christians who have the same contempt for other human beings, and who treat them as being expendable.

Had we, who claim to love God, shown more real love and understanding, more patience, more trust of others, the churches would not be vilified as they are today. I have nothing but sympathy with those who are here today and whose grief we share. I have nothing but revulsion for the less-than-human act of murder, which has so horrified us all.

I have nothing but amazement at the silence of so many of the political leaders of the world. I have nothing but sadness that our churches have failed so badly to practice what we preach. May God forgive us all, and may he bring all those who died so suddenly and unprepared into the light of His glorious presence.

Amen

* The British Prime Minister at the time of this Sermon
** Jimmy Carter
*** World Council of Churches

Acknowledgments

Field Marshal Sir Gerald Templer once wrote "Reasons for not writing my memoirs. I have never kept a Diary, nor have I kept any official documents, with three or four exceptions. It is impossible to write one's memoirs without them. One's memory can play one false so easily."

For those very same reasons, I almost never wrote this book.

This book is just a story. For the most part, it's how I remember my journey from my childhood up 'til today. I'd expect others with a shared history to have a different recollection of events – they were observing the same events through different eyes whilst being influenced by different concerns. This book is intended to entertain, amuse and inspire. If perchance, I offend or slight, it is not my intent and I apologize.

To Rebecca Ensign at Gold Leaf Press – without your patience, candor and incredible talent, translating my often-disparate ramblings into eloquent prose, this tale wouldn't have been told.

To my friends and colleagues throughout the years – without your camaraderie and influence, I wouldn't have learned, laughed, loved or cried as much.

To my ZZAM team – without your courage, kindness and willingness to chase your dreams, I wouldn't have been able to find, accept or move past my limitations.

To Mike and Ben – without your bravery on March 9th 1996, I wouldn't have lived to tell this tale.

To my family – without your acceptance, love, support, humor and all the sacrifices you've made, I wouldn't be.

To all of you and to God – thanks!